P9-DGF-207

HYMERA COMM. LIBRARY

THE BEAUTY OF
BEHOLDING
GOD

DARIEN B. COOPER

While this book is designed for the reader's personal enjoyment and profit, it is also intended for group study. A Leader's Guide with Victor Multiuse Transparency Masters is available from your local bookstore or from the publisher.

VICTOR BOOKS

a division of SP Publications, Inc.
WHEATON. ILLINOIS 60187

Offices also in Fullerton, California • Whitby, Ontario, Canada • Amersham-on-the-Hill, Bucks, England

Other books by Darien Cooper:
> *You Can Be the Wife of a Happy Husband*
> *We Became Wives of Happy Husbands*
> *Darien Cooper's Happy Husband Book*

A workbook and cassette series based on this book, and other subjects by the author, are available at your local bookstore or by writing to: His Way Library, P.O. Box 630, Buchanan, GA 30113.

Most of the Scripture quotations in this book are from the *New International Version*, © 1978 by The New York International Bible Society. Other quotations are from the *King James Version* (KJV); the *Amplified Bible* (AMP), © 1965 by Zondervan Publishing House; the *New American Standard Bible* (NASB), © 1960, 1962, 1963, 1968, 1971, 1972, 1973 by the Lockman Foundation, La Habra, California; *The Holy Bible in the Language of Today* by Dr. William F. Beck (BECK), © Mrs. William F. Beck, 1976, published by A. J. Holman Company; and *The Living Bible* (LB), © 1971 by Tyndale House. All quotations used by permission.

Recommended Dewey Decimal Classification: 248.3
Suggested Subject Headings: BEHAVIOR; CHRISTIAN LIFE; RELIGION

Library of Congress Catalog Card Number: 81-84130
ISBN: 0-88207-350-8

© 1982 by SP Publications, Inc. All rights reserved
Printed in the United States of America

VICTOR BOOKS
A division of SP Publications, Inc.
P.O. Box 1825 • Wheaton, Illinois 60187

Dedicated
to
my parents
George P. & Mildred Brown
and
my sister
Janice Lynn Bruner
whom God has used to graciously
lace my life with
love, understanding, and inspiration.

HYMERA COMM. LIBRAN

Contents

Acknowledgements

Praise God for linking our lives with others who enrich, encourage, and add a dimension and completeness that would not be there if it were not for them. Our Lord has used many in my life for that purpose and especially so in regard to this project. For each of you, I ask God's richest blessings.

With deep appreciation I say, "Thank you," to my husband, DeWitt, who has patiently and faithfully reviewed each chapter as it was written, but most of all for his tender encouragement at the beginning of this project when it seemed overwhelming to me. Also, a special thanks to him for being patient with me as I have worked through these truths in my own life and for loving me even when I do not apply what I know.

Thanks to Phyllis Ott, a dear friend, who faithfully critiqued the contents of each chapter. She dared to be honest even when she knew it would be painful and generously gave her approval and support when appropriate. Such a precious friendship is rare, and I value and appreciate it.

To Nancy Carpenter I give a gracious applause for diligently typing the final copies of each chapter even when it meant personal sacrifice to her own busy schedule. To an author who is not a typist, she was God-sent!

Thanks to Laurie Creasy for expressing in poem form my thoughts in the poem, "Just You and Me, Jesus."

Thanks, also, to another dear friend, Jackie Weidenbach, for her encouragement in the beginning of this manuscript when I was convinced that I could not communicate the truths which I felt burdened to write.

Thanks to all those who have allowed me to share their experiences as illustrations. A very special thanks to Elaine and Sarah to whom I have referred extensively throughout this book.

Introduction

How very easy and natural it is to become absorbed in problems that bombard us daily. These difficulties may range anywhere from personal turmoils, heartbreaks with our children, marital conflicts, or the world dilemmas in general. Such distresses are real. They can hurt despicably and require and deserve answers and solutions.

Time, energy, and general wear and tear can be saved if we learn to look straight through our immediate circumstances and behold our God as reigning King working everything for our good as we learn to respond to Him rather than our situation or the people involved. We look beyond the immediate to the real reason we are on Planet Earth. We see that our Lord wants to use everything that enters our lives to get us ready to live with Him as His bride forever. Our sorrows and everyday experiences are no longer wasted, but they are used to draw us into a vital love relationship with the Lord Jesus Christ in which we receive and display His very life.

As such a relationship is developed with Christ we are blessed—every aching abyss of our inner beings is satisfied—and He is honored and glorified. We learn to enjoy life and others rather than abusing them by trying to make them meet needs and function in ways they were never intended.

As I write this book I am painfully aware that I have only scratched the surface of the areas of which I write. However, I know if Jesus is lifted up and becomes our Lord and Lover, and if we seek Him with all our heart, He will make Himself known to us and bring us into a level of living far beyond our greatest expectation.

The purpose of this book is to start us on or aid us in that delightful journey back into the heart of God with Jesus as our Companion, King, Lord, Lover—our all! When He is our God, all else takes its proper perspective. Each problem, whether great or small, can be successfully worked through as we behold Him. His peace and contentment or overflowing joy will then begin saturating us as a way of life.

May I challenge you to carefully read this book from cover to cover with an open heart before our Lord Jesus Christ asking Him to minister to you before you form any conclusions about any particular sections. Please read it in the order in which it is written because one section builds upon the next.

My prayer is that all of your life will become one of living, moving and being out of, through, and to Him forever and forever! (Acts 17:27)

1
Beholding
His Overflowing Joy

The situation was critical. I was at the ripe old age of 29, and all the "I'll be happy whens" had been exhausted. My restlessness and searching were still as real as ever. The thought of passing through life and missing out on really living simply broke my heart. Ever since I could remember, I longed to live life to the fullest—to experience an overflowing joy laced with peace and contentment, with fulfillment thrown in as a bonus. Wasn't such a life promised by our God? Yes, John 15:11 described that very life. "I have told you these things that My joy and delight may be in you, and that your joy and gladness may be full measure and complete and overflowing" (AMP).

One of my "I'll be happy whens" was finding my life partner. I know God brought DeWitt and me together and I love him with all my heart. But in those early years of our marriage, it was easy for me to rationalize about our problems. I told myself that they were all his fault. I could even convince him that such was the case. The only problem was, he would not change as I suggested!

So in the meantime I sought out other "whens" for fulfillment. I convinced DeWitt that I must end my teaching career to begin our family. God graciously gave us 3 handsome boys. After the first 2 were born, the full impact of motherhood hit—and I wasn't prepared! Brian's 12 month colic was almost more than either DeWitt or I could endure. With time Brian's colic was over and our third son was well established in our family circle. But even with things running more smoothly, I realized that children were not problem-solvers. Just as I loved my husband, so I loved our boys. Nevertheless, the void remained.

God graciously used Ellie Armstrong's testimony to confirm that the overflowing joy I sought was possible. How exciting it was to read about her care for the 14 motel units she had on U.S. Route 6 in the rolling hills of western Pennsylvania. I had never been around anyone or heard of anyone who had such a sweet, moment by moment fellowship with the Lord Jesus Christ.

Through a special dedication ceremony, Ellie had set aside each of the motel rooms to God for a specific purpose: a special room for honeymooners, one for alcoholics, another for mending of broken relationships, one for spiritual conviction, one for happiness, and so on. As she entered each room in the morning to clean it before the next guest arrived, she would thank God for His presence there. As she swept, she asked God to sweep away the fears, angers, or doubts that had been left behind. While washing windows, she prayed that His light might shine into the room. And making beds became her best time with God. She said, "I've always had a bad back and making so many beds each day used to be a problem. Then I discovered that if I made beds kneeling, I wouldn't have to stoop over, and now it's the best prayer time I have!"

When a guest arrives, if his problem is not evident by observation or conversation, Ellie simply asks God which room he needs. Then she gives him the appropriate room key.

One evening God seemed to tell her to put a certain man in the room where alcoholics had often been helped, although there was nothing in his appearance to suggest this problem. Only the next morning did Ellie learn what happened.

The guest was a "cured" alcoholic who had not had a drink for two years. But that night he was despondent because he had just lost his sister to cancer. He had decided life was meaningless. He tossed his suitcase on the bed and was turning to leave the room, intending to get drunk, when he saw on the nightstand a book, *The Cross and the Switchblade*. Curiously, he picked it up. Three hours later he finished reading it. "I knelt down by the bed," he confided to Ellie the next morning, "and once again rededicated my life to God." [1]

The overflowing joy in Ellie's life was not only touching the lives of those who stayed in her motel, but it ignited a stronger thirst in me for such a life. Ellie's life revealed a walking with Jesus, a talking with Him, a fellowship that drew my heart to Him like a magnet draws steel. This had to be what I had been seeking for so long.

God seemed to be using Ellie's story along with other things to say to me, "You have sought to satisfy the inner void in your life through marriage, career, children, community and church business, social status, possessions, and even friends. Each of these was designed by Me to be enjoyed. But none of them are life-giving. Only a dependent love relationship with My Son, Jesus Christ, can infuse in and through you the overflowing joy that you've craved." This message from God was confirmed to me by Jesus' words, "I am the way and the truth and the life" (John 14:6).

Joy—What Is It?

Eagerly I began investigating this way of life—this joy—promised through Jesus. What was it? What would it mean in my life? How would it be expressed? What difference would it make in me?

Soon I discovered what God's joy was. Such joy does not necessarily refer to a state of ecstasy where one is forever giggling and laughing. *Rather, true joy means that a person is content or satisfied regardless of the problems around him.* This joy might sometimes be displayed in bursts of great gladness and delight, and at other times in a quiet sober joy that rests in a deep ocean of peace. Regardless of its expression, the person with true joy can say, "All is well in my inner being where the real me lives."

Just think! Contentment and peace despite *any problem!* That would include the turmoils of marital unfaithfulness, the loss of a partner, the emptiness of an unfulfilling marriage, the loneliness of being single, the pain brought on by rebellious children, and any other difficulty of life.

Indestructible Joy

Now I knew that the joy God promised was what my heart had sought. Pascal, the French physicist and philosopher, had accurately described my condition. "There is a God-shaped vacuum in the heart of every man which only God can fill through His Son, Jesus Christ."

With all the determination and dedication within me, I turned seeking my Lord. True to character He never turns away anyone who turns to Him. Jesus said, "If a man is thirsty, let him come to Me and drink. Whoever believes in Me, as the Scripture has said, streams of living water will flow from within him" [2] (John 7:37-38).

By turning to Jesus and beholding Him, His overflowing joy began to be a reality. I found the contentment I'd sought through a dependent love relationship with Jesus Christ, allowing His life to be my life—His joy, my joy.

I shall never forget thinking, "Oh, precious Lord, there must be something that can take away the soul-satisfying joy You have given me." It was like my Lord graciously invited me to imagine anything, then carefully examine it before Him to see if it were bigger than He, Himself.

My mind waded through the possibilities, first of all, of my greatest earthly loss . . . my beloved husband's death. Yes, no doubt I would miss him and ache for his presence. But not even his death could wipe away God's joy.

Slowly, but carefully, I considered the loss of each of our precious sons. They, too, would be missed, but the loss, I was assured, wouldn't touch God's protective presence. Next I weighed the destruction of our home and all of our possessions. Finally, I considered great pain and the loss of my personal health. Triumphantly God rose above each and every possible loss. He reassured me that nothing on Planet Earth, under the earth, or in the heavens above could separate me from His great unsurpassing love and peace.

God's Word confirmed my understanding of His everlasting love. "Who shall separate us from the love of Christ? Shall trouble or hardship or persecution or famine or nakedness or danger or sword? . . . No, in all these things we are more than conquerors through Him who loved us. For I am convinced that neither death nor life, neither angels nor demons, neither the present nor the future, nor any powers, neither height nor depth, nor anything else in all creation, will be able to separate us from the love of God that is in Christ Jesus our Lord" (Rom. 8:35-39).

The truths God made clear were almost more than I could contain. The God of heaven and earth desires to infuse our beings with His precious life. Then He reassures us in His Word that His life flowing in and through us will always be sufficient for any needs that we'll ever have. What a great God!

The psalmist provided a stimulating glimpse into the greatness of our God. "By the word of the Lord were the heavens made, their starry host by the breath of His mouth. He gathers the waters of the sea into jars; He puts the deep into storehouses" (Ps. 33:6-7).

Think about it. Our God, with the breath of His mouth, made all the stars. In our galaxy alone, the Milky Way has so many stars that counting them is impossible. For instance, if a man were to count the stars at the rate of 200 per minute, it would take him 1,000 years. Our highly specialized scientists with their modern instruments estimate that there must be more than 100 billion stars in our galaxy. Yet God "determines and counts the number of the stars; He calls them all by their names" (Ps. 147:4, AMP).

If that isn't enough to melt your heart before Him, consider that scientists have estimated that beyond our galaxy there are trillions of galaxies of which ours is average.[3] Isaiah adds to the wonder of God, "Who has measured the waters in the hollow of His hand, marked off the heavens with a nine inch span?" (Isa. 40:12, AMP)

After meditating on these facts, I responded by crying out to God, "Show me Your ways, O Lord, teach me Your paths; guide me in Your truth and teach me, for You are God my Saviour, and my hope is in You all day long" (Ps. 25:4-5).

Thirst Through Needs

God's ways were becoming clearer. He often uses needs to stir within us a thirst for Himself that only He can satisfy. God desires to use our needs to force us to look beyond the things from which we have previously sought meaning, such as relationships and possessions. Our needs are designed to be our friends—and thus should be welcomed!

God may be using a need in your life right now to draw you to Himself. Perhaps you just had not recognized it as a thirst for Him. Let Him gently guide you to live as you were created to live—in an awareness of His presence, completely dependent on Him, overflowing with His joy. The psalmist verifies that this is where real living takes place. "You will show me the path of life; in Your presence is fullness of joy, at Your right hand there are pleasures for evermore" (Ps. 16:11, AMP).

Through my needs—marital problems, inability to be a good mother, and difficulties with interpersonal relationships—God stirred up a thirst for Himself. When I turned to Him and Him alone, He met my needs. As my dependent love relationship with Him grows, I am learning to enjoy, appreciate, and relate to others in a fresh, new, and beautiful way. Life is fulfilling. It overflows with the joy His Word promises.

The following poem, "Just You and Me, Jesus," summarizes the life that began unfolding for me:

> Keep my feet upon the path
> Where we alone can walk;
> Stay my mind upon those words
> That we alone can talk.
>
> Then I won't require so much
> Of those with whom I live,
> Demanding that they must provide
> What only You can give.
>
> Freedom came the day I learned
> That You are all I need.
> As You ordain my every step,
> My every thought You read.
>
> The highest mountain I would climb
> You're there along the way,
> To still my trembling heart and hand
> Lest off the path I stray.
>
> When in the valleys I must trod,
> Not knowing where they'll end,
> I hear Your calming peaceful voice
> Your strength and love to lend.

What a joy does life become!
What treasure does it hold!
What beauty You reveal to me!
What priceless wealth untold!

I often whisper in my joy,
Or pain that's bittersweet,
The words, "Just You and me, Jesus,"
Make my life complete!

Do you desire to have peace and contentment regardless of your situation? Does your heart hunger and thirst after God? If not, bow before Him now asking that He give you that thirst. If you are already thirsty, praise Him because you are already on your way to beholding Him and enjoying His life. He *will* satisfy all those who come to Him and drink.

Notes

[1] Catherine Marshall, *God's Word Is Where You Are* (Carmel, N. Y.: Guideposts Associates, Inc.), pp. 12-15.

[2] Do you know the One who satisfies with living water? Do you know the One who gives meaning and purpose to life? If you were to die within the hour, do you know for certain that you would go to heaven? Here's how you can:

A. Heaven or eternal life is a free gift. It cannot be earned or deserved. "The wages of sin is death, but the gift of God is eternal life through Jesus Christ our Lord" (Rom. 6:23, KJV).

B. Man is a sinner and cannot save himself. "For all have sinned and come short of the glory of God" (3:23, KJV).

C. God is merciful and doesn't want to punish us, but because He is just, He must punish sin. Christ, the infinite God-Man, purchased a place in heaven for you which comes with eternal life. He did so by suffering your hell for you. "He made Him who knew no sin to be sin on our behalf, that we might become the righteousness of God in Him" (2 Cor. 5:21, NASB).

D. Man must individually receive Jesus Christ as Saviour and

Lord by faith. Faith is not mere intellectual assent, but means trusting or relying on Jesus Christ alone for salvation. "But as many as received Him, to them He gave the right to become children of God, even to those who believe in His name" (John 1:12, NASB). "That if you confess with your mouth Jesus as Lord, and believe in your heart that God raised Him from the dead, you shall be saved" (Rom. 10:9, NASB).

E. Now is the time of salvation. Don't delay. Take Christ right now and have the assurance that you have His life, eternal life, and a place with Him in heaven. Use the following prayer as a guide or use your own words. Your heart's response is the issue, not your words.

Lord Jesus Christ, I know that I am a sinner and I ask You to forgive me of my sins. Thank You for the blood You shed on Calvary to wash me clean from my sins. By faith I ask You to come into my life and be my Saviour and Lord. From this moment on, by God's grace, I am willing to follow and obey You as the Lord of my life. Thank You for coming into my heart. Amen.

F. You can *KNOW* you have eternal life and a place in heaven based on God's Word, not on your feelings or experience. "These things I have written to you who believe in the name of the Son of God, in order that *you may know* that you have eternal life" (1 John 5:13, NASB). (Here and in subsequent Scripture quotations, italics are used for author's emphasis.)

³ A. O. Schnabel, *Has God Spoken?* (San Diego: Creation Life), pp. 14-15.

2
The Beginning
of Beholding

It was a quiet Sunday afternoon in the dead of winter. The year was 1971. I was scurrying around in my own delightful, cheery world. DeWitt's calm, softly spoken words were more devastating to me than if the den roof had split wide open channeling in a bolt of lightning.

"Darien, you go your way from now on and I'll go mine. I don't want to interfere with your life, but it's clear our two worlds do not fit together. So you do your thing and I'll do mine. We just won't attempt to do them together any more!"

I couldn't believe it! What was wrong? I thought everything, well *almost* everything, was just perfect. What was he saying? I knew DeWitt didn't mean a legal divorce. But it was clear that he was describing a mental, emotional, and physical divorce. To me this was the worse of the two evils. Why? Because that would mean hypocrisy or pretending.

At that time, we were both on Campus Crusade for Christ Associate Lay Ministry Staff. We were teaching weekend seminars together, and I was teaching a women's weekly neighborhood Bible study. DeWitt wasn't saying he'd stop teaching Lay Seminars. Just that we'd do them at different times from now on. His desire was for our worlds not even to touch any more!

I simply could not accept what he was saying. His suggestion would mean that Jesus wasn't the answer for every problem—and I couldn't live with that. Either Jesus was the way, the truth, and the life, or He wasn't. I had been liberated from too many years of pretending. I wasn't about to be shackled with that bondage again. I knew it would kill me.

So adamant was I that Jesus was the answer to everything that I had not been able to forget a recent speaker's comment. He'd said, "I am sick and tired of hearing Christian speakers glibly and simplistically say, 'Christ is the answer.' " Then he had continued almost sarcastically with, "What are the questions anyway?" I wanted to shout, "It doesn't matter what the questions are. He's the answer!" And I believed it with all my being.

My quiet Sunday afternoon was turned into the greatest turmoil I'd faced up to that time. I had to grapple with the facts staring me in the face. If Christ is the answer, His solutions have to work in every area of one's life. I already knew He was who He said He was. My life had been turned upside down and inside out. There was a peace, contentment, and overflowing joy I had never before known. But how did this problem fit in?

For the first time in our marriage, I cried out, "Lord Jesus, show me how to be the wife DeWitt needs!" For the first time I was willing to seek reasons for our marital problems rather than just passing them all off on DeWitt. How I had ruined things, I didn't know. My actions had not been intentional, but it was obvious that they had been disastrous.

The direction I had chosen had been so easy to take. I was already seeing success in a teaching ministry with women. Encouragement came from everywhere that this should be the primary emphasis in my life. Now, these exact words were never spoken, but definitely implied. After all, weren't many people's lives being changed?

As I look back, it is clear that the only way I handled the shock and succeeding hurt, then applied the truths God revealed to me,[1] was by knowing how to and continuing to behold Him.

Learning to live in an awareness of God's presence, overflowing with His joy, comes as we learn to behold our God. As we behold Him, we become like Him, and are empowered to carry out the necessary changes He shows us must take place. A major change in my life was to learn to be the companion my husband needed. "But we all with open face beholding as in a glass the glory of the Lord, are changed into the same image from glory to glory, even as by the Spirit of the Lord'' (2 Cor. 3:18, KJV).

Beholding God is not complicated. Education or background have no effect on your ability to behold Him—unless you're so dependent on your education that you cannot humbly bow before God and receive His guidance in the same way that a trusting child approaches his father. Jesus said, ''I tell you the truth, unless you change and become like little children, you will never enter the kingdon of heaven'' (Matt. 18:3).

What Is Beholding?

What does it mean to behold the Lord? It means I look through every circumstance, every person, and every possession as if they were transparent glass and see my loving, compassionate God at work. I rely on and trust in Him to bring forth His purposes for His honor and glory and my blessing. Beholding God means remembering who my marvelous God is based on His attributes and relating to life situations accordingly. To behold Him, ''we fix our eyes not on what is seen, but on what is unseen. For what is seen is temporary, but what is unseen is eternal'' (2 Cor. 4:18). ''For from Him and through Him and to Him are all things. To Him be the glory forever! Amen'' (Rom. 11:36). As I behold Him, my life will be totally dependent on and abandoned to Him with a heart that responds to Him in worship.

Another way of stating the same truth is set forth in Hebrews 12:1-2. ''Let us strip off and throw aside every encumbrance . . . and let us run with patient endurance . . . the appointed course of the race that is set before us, looking away (from all that will distract) to Jesus . . .'' (AMP).

One would think that beholding our Lord would be easy. But because of our fallen state we are easily distracted and drawn away from beholding Him.

Beholding—Original State

Adam and Eve were originally created with nothing to distract them from beholding God. His life flowed through them, satisfying all their inner longings and enabling them to completely enjoy their relationship with each other.

In other words, Eve never had any problem being a helpmate, a loving companion to Adam. She naturally beheld God, received His life, and displayed it to Adam. What the Lord was to her in her inner invisible relationship with Him, she in turn lived out with Adam in her visible outward relationship. It was as natural as breathing air. She enjoyed life—His life flowing in and through her. She enjoyed being Adam's companion. Their worlds meshed into one just as their relationship with each other echoed a "oneness."

With Adam and Eve, the first married couple, there were no conflicts of interest or opposing directions emerging. With Eve it was not a matter of who was most important in her life—her Lord or her husband. Because the Lord God was her life the natural overflow was that her earthly affairs were centered around Adam and how she might please him. (See Gen. 2:18; 1 Cor. 7:34b.)

I had not learned to do this in my marriage. I had learned to develop the inner invisible relationship with Jesus, thus the overflowing joy. But I had not learned how to repeat that in my relationship with DeWitt.

Adam and Eve's world was not just made up of each other. They had their occupations through which to release their creativity. What all this encompassed we are not told. We know Adam spent time naming the animals God had created (Gen. 2:19-20). How Eve spent her spare time we don't know. But we do know there was no competing, only completing.

Beholding—Interrupted

What happened to interrupt the life-flowing love relationship that Adam and Eve experienced with their God and with each other? They stopped beholding God! They were separated from Him. They began to doubt His love and His plan for their lives and made choices independent of Him. That was sin.

The sin which contaminated them was passed on to you and me. "Therefore as sin came into the world through one man and death as the result of sin, so death spread to all men, [no one being able to stop it or escape its power] because all men sinned" (Rom. 5:12, AMP). Before sin entered the picture, Adam and Eve's spirits flowed with their Lord's Spirit receiving and displaying His glory, His very soul-satisfying life. Their spirits were channeled through their souls and displayed through their bodies.

How did this work? When the spirit was communicating love, for instance, it channeled itself through the soul allowing the mind to think love thoughts and the emotions to feel love responses. The body then manifested love actions.

As Adam and Eve lived in this perfect functioning order they rested in God, knowing that all comes from Him, is accomplished through Him, and done unto Him. Just as a fish glides through the water which surrounds it and flows through it giving life, so we are to rest in our God who surrounds us and desires to flow in and through us sustaining and being our very life. Take a fish out of its life support, water, and lay it on the dry bank, and it begins to die. Separate us from God and we too experience death—spiritual death. Adam and Eve's spiritual death, separation from God, happened immediately. Their physical deaths came years later.

Sin Reversed Our Functioning Order

Adam and Eve's sin not only separated them from God, but reversed the way they functioned. No longer were their spirits in control channeled through their souls and manifested in their bodies. Their spirits were dead Godward. The same is true of us the moment we come into the world since sin and death are passed on to us through Adam. "As for you, you were dead in your transgressions and sins, in which you used to live. . . . All of us also lived among them at one time, gratifying the cravings of our sinful nature and following its desires and thought" (Eph. 2:1-3).

The body, which was designed by God to be a display window, was now empowered by sin residing in our flesh. The body told the soul what to think (programmed the mind), regulated the emotions, and coerced the will. True life—eternal life—was cut off from man. God's life was no longer a reality or a controlling factor through our spirits. Thus a void was established in our inner beings. Without God's life flowing in and through man, the soul and body malfunctioned. Just as the inward relationship with God had deteriorated, so did the outward relationship with man.

This explains why I didn't know how to properly relate to DeWitt as his helpmate. I could not be the mother of our three sons my heart told me I should be. I was beginning to understand why I had so much tension, strain, and uneasiness in many other relationships.

Our Functioning Order Restored

The functioning order of my being needed to be restored to operate as God had originally designed. Actually, the restoration could be compared to the potter's remaking of the spoiled vessel as described by Jeremiah. "Whenever the thing the potter made was spoiled in his hands, he remade it into a new object just as he meant to make it" (Jer. 18:4, BECK).

Just as the vessel is completely pliable in the potter's hands, so we must learn to totally yield to God and allow Him to remake us as He sees fit. Our minds, which have been programmed by our sinful natures, must be reprogrammed so that we think the way God thinks. " 'For My thoughts are not your thoughts, neither are your ways My ways,' declares the Lord" (Isa. 55:8). Our emotions must be trained to respond to our spirits rather than allowing them to make us a slave to our feelings. We learn to commit our will to God's will rather than being swept along by the power of sin.

Knowing that God was using my marital problems as well as other difficult situations to remake me made my struggles exciting. There *was* a purpose—a reason behind it all. I began to see through the immediate problems, as they appeared to be, to the spiritual understanding that they were benefiting me not only for eternity but for now!

Our time spent here on earth can be viewed as a dress rehearsal. We might even describe it as boot camp when the going gets rough. Regardless, we can shout with Paul, "Thanks be to God! He gives us the victory through our Lord Jesus Christ. Therefore, my dear brothers, stand firm. Let nothing move you. Always give yourselves fully to the work of the Lord, because you know that your labor in the Lord is not in vain" (1 Cor. 15:57-58).

Beholding from Glory to Glory

As we learn to behold God then respond to others as He directs, our functioning order begins to be reversed so that we live as designed.

We are fulfilled and God is honored. From 2 Corinthians 3:18, quoted in the beginning of this chapter, we read that such growth is from glory to glory. It is a gradual process which takes time.

How does this work in daily living? For instance, let us take the common problem of anger. When I hear angry words coming out of my mouth, at first my soul may realize only enough of the sense of God to know that my angry emotions, empowered by sin, are in charge. Then I learn to apply some basic truths taught in God's Word. I am to be controlled by the Spirit. And to "ever be filled and stimulated with the [Holy] Spirit" (Eph. 5:18, AMP). My angry words show that my sinful nature is in control and not the Holy Spirit. (See Galatians 5:19-26.) What do I do? I apply another scriptural principle. "If we confess our sins, He is faithful and just and will forgive us our sins and purify us from all unrighteousness" (1 John 1:9).

As we respond to the realization God gives us at this stage, He then is able to take us farther. Gradually, as we obediently confess our sins each time He shows them to us and again turn to Him trusting Him to flow through us by faith, we will begin to recognize the fruit of the flesh in our thoughts before they are expressed in words. We, then, progress to trusting Him for our thoughts.

As we grow stronger spiritually, our angry thoughts will come less often, thus that problem gradually decreases. Not only do we learn how to respond to the sins in our lives, but we learn how to behold God in different ways and in various stages of maturity. With each new understanding comes a greater love for God. That is what is meant from stage to stage or glory to glory.

Beholding—Key to Victory

Beholding my God in and through all things that happen is the key to living as God intended—in His presence overflowing with joy. As we learn to behold Him as a way of life, we can work through any problem regardless of its intensity and come through to victory.

Beholding Jesus has been the key to marital peace in my relationship with DeWitt. Today we know a sweeter intimacy than I ever dreamed possible. Yes, we are still learning and growing. I humbly thank DeWitt for being so patient with me as I have worked through and continue to work through my weaknesses.

HYMERA COMM. LIBRARY

You might be thinking, "Your problems weren't as tragic as mine. How can I know that what you're saying is the answer for me too?" Good point. Let's let others speak.

Sarah also testifies to victory in her torn life through beholding her Lord. She is learning to look straight through her circumstances to see her Lord's loving compassion bringing forth His purpose in her life. Many people would say that is impossible knowing the odds against her. Sarah's husband left her to live with another woman. During this time Sarah gave birth to their fourth child. She was further humiliated by having to leave a beautiful home and her middle-class lifestyle to live in a low-rent apartment project accepting welfare.

Sarah prayed and prayed for her husband's return, thinking victory could never be known till he came back. Then one day when baring her soul before the Lord, Sarah knew and embraced victory. Peace, joy, contentment, and fulfillment were not dependent on circumstances or people, but on beholding God.

Sarah continues working through many facets of her life as God deals with her. The changes aren't easy or sudden. Later we will see how she worked through areas that haunt us all. How she claimed and maintains her victory. Sarah knows that beholding her Lord is the key to working out every difficult situation.

Sarah's situation is not an isolated case. Elaine is another dear friend who has faced the worst and yet found victory through beholding the Lord. Elaine's husband, who has his own law practice, became involved with his secretary. At first he was merely a concerned friend to a woman who had many problems. But before long, his compassion led him into a carefully spun web designed by the secretary to break up his Christian home. After a series of heartbreaking circumstances, he married the secretary.

Elaine was left with three teenage children, a broken home, and a shattered home church situation. Who could blame her for being bitter, resentful, and vindictive? Elaine struggled with all those things in her legitimate hurt and came through to victory. As with Sarah, later on we will see how Elaine worked through these areas. But today she, too, claims victory through beholding Jesus!

Regardless of the uniqueness of your personal situation, the solution is the same—beholding God and obeying what He shows you through His power. Pause for a moment and consider that God's timetable for bringing you to victory is just as perfect as His timetable for His celestial bodies.

"Halley's comet, probably the best known of all the great comets, was last seen in the spring and summer of 1910. It is slated to reappear in 1986. During the 76 years in which it will be out of sight on earth it will travel a total of 3 billion miles, which will take it far beyond the most distant planets of Uranus, Neptune, and Pluto. And yet, by their mathematical calculations, astronomers are absolutely sure of its reappearance on accurate schedules in 1986, as it has always appeared on schedule in previous intervals of 76 years.

"Consider what this means! During that period of 76 years, this comet is now traveling without stopping for refueling or repairs, a distance of 3 billion miles. Yet we can be sure it will arrive exactly on schedule according to its fixed timetable." [2]

Let God use that which we can see, such as Halley's comet, to encourage us to believe Him for what we cannot see. Then pray the following prayer (or a similar one of your own): *Father, I bow before You thanking You that Your plan for my life is perfect. You are bringing it to pass according to Your timetable. I trust You for me and my loved ones.*

Notes

[1] These truths are set forth in my book, *You Can Be the Wife of a Happy Husband* (Victor). This author is assuming that the truths of helping your husband like himself through praise and admiration, accepting him as he is, letting him be number one above all other earthly relationships, and submitting to his leadership and protection as unto the Lord are already becoming a reality in your life. If not, the above book is a must reading.

[2] Alfred M. Rehwinkel, *The Wonders of Creation* (Grand Rapids: Baker), pp. 149-150.

3
Beholding
Him Through
Creation

Since beholding God is the way we are changed from one degree of glory to another, it is imperative that we learn to see His glory as manifested around us. We can begin by developing an awareness of Him. What better place to start developing "God-conscious eyes" than by seeing Him through His creation.

Shortly after moving to the country, Ken, our younger son, who is very interested in hunting and observing the ways of animals, pointed out a mother quail and her little ones strutting across the field. Many landmarks and directives had to be given before my insensitive eyes spotted the family of quail. Other times he has spotted squirrels scampering from tree to tree when I was not aware any were within miles. During a long walk in the woods, he can point out such things as where deer bed down, where their active trails are, where the bucks mark off areas as their territories, and where they eat. He has "country eyes" that are trained to detect and observe animals because that is what interests him. Let us set our minds on seeing God's infinite glory as revealed in the heavens, the earth, and all that is in heaven and thereby developing "God-conscious" eyes. Once we develop a consciousness of Him in nature, it will be easy to apply His same wonderful love and care to our personal situations.

Beholding Him in Space
Let's begin by taking a trip through space traveling at the speed of light—186,000 miles per second. This means we would be cruising

26

along at approximately 670 million miles per hour. We could move across the 49 million miles separating us from Mars in about 4½ minutes.

If we keep on moving in our journey toward Jupiter which is only 390 million miles from earth, we'd arrive in 35 minutes. Next Saturn could be seen out our side window in only 71 minutes after leaving the earth some 793 million miles away. As we approached Saturn our attention would be quickly drawn to the rings around this planet which reach some 80,000 miles out from Saturn giving a halo appearance. No other planet has such rings.

Then focusing our attention just ahead of us, some 1 billion 689 million miles from Earth, we would spot Uranus and actually arrive there in approximately another hour and 20 minutes. Neptune would be next on our itinerary, some 2 billion 700 million miles from earth.

Finally, Pluto would be next enroute. After traveling some 3 billion 577 million miles from earth for approximately 5 hours and 20 minutes, we would reach the farthest planet in our solar system.

After traveling so very far we would have only taken the first step off the front porch of space because we would not have gotten out of our tiny, little solar system which moves in a multi-million mile orbit through space.[1] The nearest star, Alpha Centauri, is so far that its light, traveling at our same speed of 186,000 miles per second, takes 4.3 years to reach the earth. There are considered to be billions of stars in our galaxy alone. The star, Betelgeuese, which is about 70 times farther away than Alpha Centauri, has an average diameter greater than the orbits of Mercury, Venus, Earth, and Mars.[2] At this point we will stop because by this time numbers begin to spin around in our minds losing their meaning.

Beholding Him in the Heavens

Let's see what God says about the heavens, keeping in mind that we have gotten only a glimpse into a very minute portion of His universe. "The heavens declare the glory of God; the skies proclaim the work of His hands. Day after day they pour forth speech; night after night they display knowledge. There is no speech or language where their voice is not heard. Their voice goes out into all the earth, their words to the ends of the world" (Ps. 19:1-4).

Every minute detail of creation was fashioned by the hand of God and reveals His glory. "When I consider Your heavens, the work of Your fingers, the moon and the stars, which You have set in place . . . O Lord, our Lord, how majestic is Your name in all the earth!" (8:3, 9) The psalmist states that the heavens, the moon, and the stars are the work of God's fingers. The word translated *the work of God's fingers* is used elsewhere in the Old Testament for embroidery work. It was used in connection with the tabernacle for the embroidered tapestries that formed the veil between the holy place and the holy of holies. It was the work of an artisan's fingers. When the psalmist looked at the vast starry heavens, he exclaimed that this was God's handiwork!

Angels seem to have no trouble beholding God through His handiwork. Listen to their response as they observed His limitless power displayed in creation. "The morning stars sang together and all the angels shouted for joy" (Job 38:7).

Such a great God! When I meditate on these momentous facts about God, trying to grasp the Person behind such a creation, my mind strains . . . struggles . . . and collapses! All I can do is behold Him in awe and adoration! Then I bow before Him in love saying, "I trust in You, O Lord; I say, 'You are my God.' For the sake of Your name lead and guide me" (Ps. 31:14, 3).

Remember that everything in the universe reflects the glory of God for those with God-conscious eyes. No longer will you think of a star as being merely a flaming ball of gas. You will know that is only what it is made of. Actually it is a declaration of God's glory. Never again allow yourself to gaze into the heavens and only see objects of creation, but see your Creator displaying His glory and adore Him!

Upon rising each morning, learn to behold the new sunrise that your God has painted in the sky. No longer will you just be reminded that the sun is a mass of incandescent gas; a gigantic nuclear furnace where hydrogen is built into helium at a temperature of millions of degrees. Such heat is so great that a pinhead covered with the material at the core of the sun would give off enough heat to kill a man one million miles away.

As you observe the sunrise, lift your heart to God, praising Him for the witness the sun's pouring forth on the earth is of His power and faithfulness. It demonstrates that our God is in command and is shouting out to us of His faithfulness to fulfill His promises in our lives. We see this in God's conversation with Job and His promise to David. "Have you ever given orders to the morning or shown the dawn its place? The earth takes shape like clay under a seal; . . . His line will continue forever and his throne endure before me like the sun; it will be established forever like the moon, the faithful witness in the sky" (Job 38:12, 14; Ps. 89:36-37).

As God's faithfulness fills our minds as demonstrated to us through the sun's regular performance, our own faithlessness and that of others around us will take its proper perspective. We will know He is great enough to absorb it all. But contentment comes from being occupied with Him first and foremost, then relating to our problems, not vice versa.

Beholding Him in the Elements

Look at water. Learn to no longer simply see a combination of hydrogen and oxygen. Instead see an incredible mixture in just the right proportion to serve man's needs displaying another of God's crowning miracles. Praise God as you daily enjoy liquid refreshment without which your body could not exist. His provision is gracious! There is ample reason whichever way we turn to observe His glory when we look for it.

Note the many ways God uses water and rejoice at His display of wisdom. What a joy it is for me to walk through the grass early on a clear summer morning, and marvel at the tiny, glistening drops of water on the blades of grass. Then to respond to God with, "Father, only You could conceive of such wonders. Today I open up my heart, soul, and mind to You. Cause me to love You without reservation." Because I behold my Lord through the dew on the grass, it is easier to greet my family with the love of God flowing through my being.

Then, a few months later in the fall, I notice the same blades of grass are no longer covered with dew, but now are painted with artistic formations of lacy ice crystals called frost. What a God of love to create such a masterpiece of beauty, wonder, and variation so that we could behold Him.

As I gaze into the pulsating, rolling waves lapping on the seashore at the ocean's edge, reverence for God comes forth. Think about what He has done. "I made the sand a boundary for the sea, an everlasting barrier it cannot cross. The waves may roll, but they cannot prevail; they may roar, but they cannot cross it" (Jer. 5:22). Tiny grains of sand so light they can be carried by the wind hold the world's oceans in their boundaries because God sets them up as a barrier. There are about 326 million cubic miles of water covering nearly three-fourths of the earth's surface. Upon such realization I lift my heart to God crying out, "My God and my Lord, I adore You! I lay my life before You."

When one drop of rain splatters on my face, I ponder the miracle of God's workings. He has brought about the phenomenon of the earth's rain cycle. Taking sea water which is 800 times heavier than air and vaporizing it by the sun's rays, He makes it lighter than air and draws it into the atmosphere leaving the salt behind.

As the sun shines on the ocean's surface, it draws into the upper atmosphere about 5,435 tons of water per square mile of ocean surface. This vapor rises to considerable heights, then moves, by means of air currents, across the continents. When this warm, vapor-saturated air cools, it condenses into innumerable tiny droplets so small that about 8 million are needed to make a single drop of rain! As this condensation occurs, clouds are formed; and as the air cools, the tiny droplets fuse into larger drops till the air is unable to support them. The larger drops reach the earth in the form of rain.[3] Only our God is the Father of such wonders and it's to our advantage to behold His glory in it all as we adore Him. "Does the rain have a father? Who fathers the drops of dew? . . . Who gives birth to the frost from the heavens?" (Job 38:28-29) Let your heart sing with mine, "He's my Father, my Lord, and my Saviour."

Beholding Him in the Reptiles

God's creation seems inexhaustible in its uniqueness, creativity, and variety. Take the turtle. It is a creature quite distinct from all other forms of marine life—neither fish nor fowl. The sea is the natural habitat of the turtle, but to propagate its kind the turtle leaves the sea, migrates to the land to lay its eggs, and then returns to the sea.

God's perfect programming of these creatures shows up in their migration of great distances over the sea. A few years ago a sea captain caught a large green turtle off the coast of Nicaragua. He marked this turtle and then shipped it to Florida, about 800 miles away. There it was set free and returned to the ocean. Eight months later, the same turtle was caught at exactly the same place where it had been captured the first time. Without compass or radar, this awkward creature had traveled 800 miles across an uncharted sea and had found its way back to the very spot where it had been hatched in the first place.[4] This creature provides us with a glimpse into the wondrous and mind-boggling ways of our Creator. My heart is reassured once again that my God reigns and that every area of my life is carefully planned for and guided by Him.

Beholding Him in the Birds

As we observe God's character through His creation, we cannot help but notice the birds. Our natural tendency is to behold men rather than God. But when we take an honest appraisal of the handiwork of each bird there is no doubt where our allegiance belongs. It took man nearly 6,000 years to learn to fly. But God's airplanes have been flying ever since the fifth day of creation. They require no elaborate factory to produce them, no skilled engineer to build them. The old reproduce themselves by merely laying a few eggs and hatching them, and in a few weeks the new model takes to the air. Each has his own built-in pilot and needs no compass or radar. They require no runway to take off, and can stop in an instant wherever they happen to be.

For example, the peregrine falcon can dive on its prey at speeds up to 180 miles an hour, yet it remains under perfect control. The little hummingbird can travel 60 miles an hour and is able to fly backwards, sideways, and hover helicopter-like in midair. This little creature is able to fly nonstop the 500 miles across the Gulf of Mexico to South America. What man has designed a jet, such as God's birds, that needs no refueling and no mechanical checkups?

The swallows' regular and punctual return to Capistrano each year March 19th continues to fascinate me. Each year the waiting tourists observe their arrival from Argentina some 9,000 miles away where they have spent the winter. The swallows are always on time, not a day late or early, and precisely on course!

Those of us who are learning to see God in and through His creation begin to be aware of the one true God who is tender, loving, and very compassionate. "Look at the birds of the air; they do not sow or reap or store away in barns, yet your heavenly Father feeds them. Are you not much more valuable than they?" (Matt. 6:26)

Consider the sparrows. Most people pay very little attention to them because they don't compare in beauty to the other birds. Actually, they are often thought of as pests. But what does God say about them? "Are not five sparrows sold for two pennies? Yet not one of them is forgotten by God" (Luke 12:6).

Learning to open our eyes to behold God's glory leaves us with an awareness of His love. We begin to feel as the little boy whose father wanted to teach him about God's love. He took him to the top of a high hill and pointed northward over Scotland, southward over England, eastward over the ocean, westward over hill and valley, and then sweeping his arm around the whole circling horizon, he said, "Johnny, my son, God's love is as big as all that." "Why, Father," the little boy replied with sparkling eyes, "then we must be right in the middle of it."

Seeing the beauty of the Lord is what we have been doing as we examined His creation. This is what we are doing when we develop God-conscious eyes. His beauty satisfies and fulfills our inner beings. Join with David in his request to God, "One thing I ask of the Lord, this is what I seek: that I may dwell in the house of the Lord all the days of my life, to gaze upon the beauty of the Lord and to seek Him in His temple" (Ps. 27:4).

God's Masterpiece—His Family

Now let's consider God's creation that to some is the most astounding—the angels. Upon close examination we learn that they are indescribably beautiful, majestic, powerful, and intelligent. They rule celestial domains of untold magnitude and of inconceivable grandeur. They surround the throne of the Almighty and make up the court of the King of kings. They are so exalted as to hover over the throne of the Most High. Their countenance is so magnificent and their presence so commanding that we might be tempted to fall down to worship them if we weren't warned not to. In view of all of this, it would be easy to reason: the angels are God's masterpieces—the greatest of all display of His glory.

However, wonder of all wonders, the highest ranking angel is outranked by the most insignificant human being who has trusted Christ as his Saviour. Any redeemed human being has become, reverently speaking, the "next of kin" to the Trinity. We are children of God. "How great is the love the Father has lavished on us, that we should be called children of God! And that is what we are!" (1 John 3:1)

Unlike the angels or any other created thing, we are given the honor of all honors. What a privilege to have the very life of God flowing in and through us. "For you have been born again, not of perishable seed, but of imperishable" (1 Peter 1:23). "Everyone who believes that Jesus is the Christ is born of God" (1 John 5:1). "No one who is born of God will continue to sin, because God's seed remains in him" (1 John 3:9). God has made us "partakers of the divine nature" (2 Peter 1:4, KJV). Yes, the Father through His Son Jesus Christ, elevated us beyond the angels in the radiant canopy of the firmament.

Jesus reminds us that He is not ashamed to call us family! He says He is our brother. "But we see Jesus, who was made a little lower than the angels, now crowned with glory and honor because He suffered death, so that by the grace of God He might taste death for everyone. Both the one who makes men holy and those who are made holy are of the same family. So Jesus is not ashamed to call them brothers" (Heb. 2:9, 11). After Jesus had tasted death for us, He referred to His Father as our Father also. This He did in speaking to Mary when she was searching for Him at the empty tomb. Never before had Jesus made this assertion. "I am returning to My Father and your Father, to My God and your God" (John 20:17).

As if being children of the most high and true God and having Jesus as our brother is not enough, we are also heirs of God and coheirs with Christ. "Now if we are children, then we are heirs—heirs of God and coheirs with Christ, if indeed we share in His sufferings in order that we may also share in His glory" (Rom. 8:17).

What God has done for us is so phenomenal our finite minds simply cannot grasp it. Only He can open up our understanding and help us begin to comprehend the magnitude of it all. Join with me in a prayer that has been mine for some time now. It's Paul's prayer for the Christians in Ephesus. "I pray also that the eyes of your heart may be enlightened in order that you may know the hope to which He has called you" (Eph. 1:18).

The covenants God has established with man help us understand a little more of His infinite love. Actually, the whole Bible is the story of these covenants. The familiar term, Old Testament, is another way of saying Old Covenant and the New Testament is the New Covenant.

The particular covenant that excites me because of its application to us, we will call the blood covenant. We see this agreement first being entered into by God and Abram. Carefully read Genesis 15. Before we examine what this meant to Abram and now to us, perhaps we would understand more vividly if we see what a binding strong covenant this is when taken by two mere imperfect human beings.

When two people become brothers by blood covenant, they can never be parted. It is the strongest bond known joining the two parties into an indissolvable union. The details of entering such a covenant vary across the world, but all share the same basic ideas. Through a ceremony the two parties come together, shed, and mingle their blood. Often this is done by the cutting of the wrists and allowing the blood to run down. Then raising their right hands they swear to each other all that they are. From that day forward they share each other's strengths, weaknesses, fortunes, and failures. What happens to one is the same as happening to the other. One's debts become the other's debts, just as one's good fortune is the other's good fortune. To hurt one is to hurt the other, to bless one is to honor the other.

The resultant scar from the flesh wound is carried in their bodies forever as a reminder of their oneness. They would even change their names and be publicly known as covenant blood brothers. If Tom Smith became John Brown's blood brother, their new names would be Tom Brown Smith and John Smith Brown. The ceremony is closed by a meal enjoyed together.

When God makes a covenant with man, a problem arises that is not present when two people make a covenant. Man comes to man on an equal basis. But we, like Abram, are not on an equal basis with God. He is the Creator and we are the creatures. We are sinners and He is the holy One.

How is it possible for Him to enter into a binding, indissolvable union with us who are not equal with Him or of the same mind? Through the miracle of the Incarnation. God became flesh and dwelt among men. The one person, Jesus Christ the Son of God, represented the whole human race and at the same time was on an equal basis with the Father. He entered into a covenant with God in our place just as He did for Abram (Gen. 15:17-18). We, like Abram, can do nothing but believe. "Abram believed the Lord, and He credited it to him as righteousness" (v. 6).

The word *believe* means to rest in the work of another, to give oneself up, surrender to another, to say the Amen.[5] Just as Abraham's part of the covenant was to give himself totally to God, so must we. Likewise, just as God was bound in covenant to be Abraham's righteousness, shield, protection, and guarantor of blessing, so is He to us. God has made us "next of kin," blood brothers with Jesus. What happened to Him, happened to us. What happens to us, happens to Him. He is in us and we are in Him. What privileged people we are!

In His Image

As we behold God's creation and ourselves in particular, the picture becomes more and more exciting. God says when we trust in Jesus Christ as our personal Saviour, we become a completely new, unique, and exclusive order of beings. "When someone becomes a Christian, he becomes a brand new person inside. He is not the same any more. A new life has begun!" (2 Cor. 5:17, LB) This new order of beings has not only been placed in a very intimate kinship with the Creator God, but they can now fulfill the purpose for which they were created—to reflect God's glory.

We, of all creation, were created in His image! "So God created man in His own image, in the image of God He created him" (Gen. 1:27). God said this one will be unlike the animals, plants, and the planets. This one will be a copy of us! We have similarities to the animals—we eat food, drink water, and need sleep just like they do. But we are not of the animal class. We are a reflection of God. He is the voice and we are the echo.

Another way of illustrating this beautiful truth is to compare a Christian to a glass prism. Without light, a prism really is not much at all—just a hunk of glass. But with light, it reflects all the colors of the rainbow. The brand new persons we are now in Christ are like flawless prisms designed by the Creator. We receive His very life (invisible to the world) and translate that light into the visible colors of the character of God.

We receive, transform, and display the otherwise invisible glories of the infinite God into limitless, visible colors—the rainbow of His own attributes so that all creation might see God. His love, His power, His beauty, His patience are all shown forth through us. We are a manifestation of the "fruit of the Spirit!" [6] (See Gal. 5:22-23.) "But we have this treasure in jars of clay to show that this all-surpassing power is from God and not from us" (2 Cor. 4:7).

As we behold our Lord, whether through His creation or by other means, He is able to restore us to God's image in which we were originally created. In other words, Jesus came to bring us back to God. Scripture confirms this. "For Christ died for sins once for all, the righteous for the unrighteous, *to bring you to God*" (1 Peter 3:18, author's emphasis added). "I am the way and the truth and the life. *No one comes to the Father except through Me*" (John 14:6, author's emphasis added). I can't think of anything more exciting than being on a journey back into the heart of God with Jesus as my leader!

Notes

[1] The miles and times were calculated from a chart in the book by Herbert S. Lim and Robert H. Baker, *Stars* (New York: Golden Press), pp. 35, 104-105.

[2] *The World Book Encyclopedia*, Vol. 17, p. 475.

[3] John D. Jess, *The Birds and the Bees* (Chicago: Moody Press), pp. 75-76.

[4] Alfred M. Rehwinkel, *The Wonders of Creation* (Grand Rapids: Baker), pp. 166-167.

[5] Malcolm Smith, *How I Learned to Meditate* (Plainfield, NJ: Logos International), p. 33.

[6] The prism concept was gleaned from David C. Needham, *Birthright* (Portland, OR: Multnomah), pp. 75, 93.

4
Beholding
Him Through
Knowing Him

"Do you know Billy Graham, Corrie ten Boom, Joni Eareckson, Dale Evans Rogers, or Edith Schaeffer?" would be a typical question asked anyone that is before the public in a speaking ministry. We are often enthralled by the "famous" or the top people of the groups we admire and somehow consider it significant if our lives have touched theirs even if it is by a second or third hand contact. I love a friend's answer to such questions when they are directed his way.

"No, but *I know God!*" he says. After they have recovered from the shock he adds, "And furthermore *He delights* in my company." His answer puts things in the proper perspective. It's easy to attach too much importance to knowing other people. Even if we did know them, we couldn't be assured that they enjoyed our company. But when we seek to know God, we have chosen the highest, most worthwhile pursuit in life, and we can likewise be assured He enjoys our company.

What a joy to turn your mind first thing each morning to God. Your eye catches a glimpse of the freshly made sunrise, the frost on the windows, and the birds flying in the air. Your heart leaps as you whisper, "Behold my God. His handiwork is magnificent!" Then your heart swells even more when you remember the verse, "You will seek Me and find Me when you seek Me with all your heart. Let not the wise man boast of his wisdom or the strong man boast of his strength or the rich man boast of his riches, but let him who boasts boast about this: that he understands and knows Me, that I am the

Lord, who exercises kindness, justice, and righteousness on earth, for in these I delight'' (Jer. 29:13; 9:23-24). My mind is set: I want to know You today, Lord. I want to know and love You more today than yesterday, but not as much as I will tomorrow. What a challenge! What an adventure!

In the late 60s, knowing God became my main pursuit. I turned to Him first thing each morning, seeking to know Him and Him alone— not His gifts, not His blessings, and not even His joy. I have never been disappointed except when I make my goal something other than knowing and beholding Him. Jesus tells us that the first and greatest commandment is to ''Love the Lord your God with all your heart and with all your soul and with all your mind'' (Matt. 22:37). When we make this our goal, ''He who believes in Him—who adheres to, trusts in and relies on Him—shall never be disappointed or put to shame'' (1 Peter 2:6, AMP).

Our Company—A Delight

The fact that God wants us to know Him and delights in our company is about more than I can fathom. Just think, the God of heaven and earth that simply spoke and the world and all therein came into existence wants our fellowship. His Word assures us this is true. ''The Lord delights in those who fear Him, who put their hope in His unfailing love'' (Ps. 147:11). Not only does He delight in us, but He wants us to delight and take pleasure in Him. ''Delight yourself in the Lord'' (37:4). John confirms that such fellowship is the source of our joy. ''We proclaim to you . . . so that you may also have fellowship with us. And our fellowship is with the Father and with His Son, Jesus Christ. We write this to make your joy complete'' (1 John 1:3-4).

The only way I can even begin to grasp God's desire to fellowship with us is to remember how much I delight in getting to know and interact with my sons. It thrills my heart to know they enjoy my company and desire to be with me. I fondly remember the times my children have opened their souls to me—letting me be a part of what they are thinking, feeling, and desiring.

Then I remember. We are God's next of kin. He loved us so much that of all creation He made us in His image. Then He did the utmost. He gave His life for us. Why? He wants our fellowship! And He has done everything possible to bring it about.

Examining the Scriptures shows that God's primary record of His relationship with man is based on those who will fellowship or walk and talk with Him. Reading Genesis 3:8, it is evident the Lord had habitually walked and talked with Adam and Eve. "Then the man and his wife heard the sound of the Lord God as He was walking in the garden in the cool of the day." We have no record of Adam and Eve fellowshipping with God after they sinned. Many genealogies later we read of another man who walked with God. "Enoch walked with God; then he was no more, because God took him away" (5:24).

The story has been told that the Lord and Enoch were walking and talking one day when Enoch said, "Lord, it is getting late. Hadn't we better start back home?" The Lord said, "We are closer to My house than yours. Why don't we just spend the night there?" Since there is no night in heaven, they are still there.

Later we read, "Noah was a righteous man, blameless among the people of his time, and he walked with God" (6:9). The Lord told Noah the exact size and how to do everything in order to build the very best ship possible. For 120 years they fellowshipped over this project. After the boat was finished they took up zoology, collecting two of each animal and storing them in the ship. Next, they went sailing. Once the crisis was over Noah turned to outward stimulation from the vine rather than the inward stimulation from the Lord. We don't read of his walking with the Lord again (Gen. 9:20-29).

Hundreds more years pass, enough to develop a dignified civilization, then we read of Abram from Ur of the Chaldees leaving his homeland to walk and talk with God.

God continued to reach out to communicate with man as we see with the children of Israel at Mount Sinai. Listen to their response to His voice. "Those who heard it begged that no further word be spoken to them" (Heb. 12:19). However, God so longed to be among His children that He gave directions for building the tabernacle so that He could dwell among them and communicate with them.

The tabernacle not only laid out the steps whereby the Israelites could approach God, but serves as a pattern. The first step was made in the outer court by coming to the brazen altar. Here Christ's work on the cross is depicted by the sacrifice. Next the laver was provided so that the priests could wash themselves of sin and worldly pollution before entering the holy place.

In the holy place, fellowship with the Lord was enjoyed. There all illumination came from the lampstand. The table of showbread held the loaves of bread which the priest ate. The altar of incense stood just in front of the veil separating the holy place from the holy of holies. There incense burned rendering a sweet aroma to God before entering the holy of holies and God's presence.

What a fortunate, privileged people we are today. The veil has been "torn in two" (Matt. 27:51), and God has made the body of each of His children His holy temple. "Do you not know that your body is a temple of the Holy Spirit, who is in you?" (1 Cor. 6:19) God desires that we, who are believer priests, minister to Him, delighting in His company as He delights in our fellowship.

Turn to Him as God

Enjoying daily fellowship with our Lord means that He must be our God. We recognize that in the Garden of Eden. Eve desired to be as God or like God rather than His creature dependent on Him. Genesis 3:5 reads, "For God knows that when you eat of it your eyes will be opened, and you will be like God." From that time on, whether consciously or unconsciously, we have presumed to be as God. We decide *what* should meet our needs, *how* it should be accomplished, and *when*. We then proceed to try to bring it about. That is what living as God or like God means.

Often *we* decide our husbands or our marriages should be the source of our fulfillment. As Sarah and I talked one day, she said, "That's exactly what I did to Steve. I tried to make him fulfill my inner needs. When he was not home on time, I complained. That was to be the highlight of my day. How dare he not do as I decided he should. When he did not give me the attention and praise I thought I needed, I grumbled, manipulated, and schemed to try to make him do so. Now I can see *I* put my husband in God's place in my life. This placed him in a role he could not fulfill. He became frustrated and so did I. I know now I was abusing our relationship rather than enjoying it by trying to sap my very life from him rather than from my relationship with Jesus."

This realization was a shock to Sarah, but it was a healthy insight. She began to see the problem and to know that her helpless dependent fellowship with Jesus was the answer.

The following questions can help us determine if *we* are acting as God, thereby deciding who or what will give us fulfillment.

1. Do you try to change your husband? If so, you may believe that you'll be fulfilled if he is different.
2. Do you try to manipulate or scheme to get your way? Such actions show that you think you'll be content only if you get your way.
3. Do you approach your role in the marriage relationship with the attitude, "I'll try this for awhile. If it doesn't produce the results I want, I'll stop." When God is your God, you do what He says as long as there is breath within you, whether or not you see desirable results.
4. Do you often experience anger, rage, and bitterness? Such emotions erupt when others fail in what you had decided they should or shouldn't do. In other words, you dared to act as God!
5. Do you readily forgive others? If not, you're saying, "You crossed MY WILL and I WILL determine what should be done."
6. Do you entertain worry and fear? If so, you're setting yourself up as God trying to decide what will happen and how to handle it.
7. Do you complain and grumble? If so, you're saying, "I want to be as God and change the way things are. I would do a better job."

We must firmly place in our minds that our strength and fulfillment come from knowing and fellowshipping with God. "The people who know their God shall prove themselves strong and shall stand firm, and do exploits [for God] (Dan. 11:32, AMP). Not only does one's strength come from knowing God, but one's very life comes from Him, and Him alone. "Now this is eternal life: that they may know You, the only true God, and Jesus Christ, whom You have sent" (John 17:3).

Our Lord reminds us that when He is in control, our inner needs will be satisfied. We will be free to enjoy others rather than abuse them. "Being with you, I desire nothing on earth" (Ps. 73:25). "You will know the truth, and the truth will set you free" (John 8:32). When He is our God, we can begin to enjoy our husbands, our children, our work, without misusing them by trying to sap life, meaning, and purpose for living from them.

Spiritual Marriage—Earthly Fulfillment

As we learn to allow God to meet needs we have previously tried to force others to meet, the satisfaction our souls have sought begins to be a reality. This fellowship is compared to the marriage relationship throughout Scripture. Israel was referred to as the wife of the Father. We are known as the bride of Christ. (See Isa. 54:5; 62:5; 2 Cor. 11:2.)

When we respond to our Lord in the intimate fellowship and oneness in which He so delights, we can legitimately say that He is our spiritual husband. By allowing Him to be our spiritual husband, we can in turn relate to our mates as their companions or close friends without trying to make them fulfill needs only Jesus can meet. Herein lies our peace, contentment, and overflowing joy whether we are married, single, divorced, or widowed.

Elaine has discovered that Jesus makes up for the void left by the absence of her husband. A few months ago she was sitting by herself in a crowd at her son's football game. For a few minutes she was overwhelmed with loneliness and a sadness that she could not share this precious time with her ex-husband. Along with this realization came floods of past memories seeking to be relived. Only a few moments passed before she knew that this time could either be spent in a first-class "pity party" or by fellowshipping with Jesus.

Turning to Jesus in the inner sanctuary of her being, she released everything to Him as her God. Her response was the same as the psalmist's: "To You, O Lord, I lift up my soul; in You I trust, O my God. According to Your love remember me, for You are good, O Lord" (Ps. 25:1-2, 7).

She looked around at the beautiful mountains covered with rich autumn leaves and started praising her Lord. She thanked Him for her wonderful son and for His graciousness in caring for them. On and on she chatted with Jesus about everything, including the details of the game, till she was lost in His care and her loneliness disappeared.

She recalled the game with fondest memories saying, "Even

though I was by myself I was not alone. It was a good time. I can't remember a time that was more exciting and fulfilling.''

One day as Sarah and I were talking she said, ''I know Jesus is to be my fulfillment and meet my needs. But why am I not fulfilled?'' Sarah was used to seeking fulfillment through her physical senses— touching, seeing, hearing, and tasting. But she was beginning to understand that fulfillment which truly satisfies begins in the inner being and is merely displayed through the physical, rather than being governed by the physical.

When God began making this lesson real to Sarah, she seemed to be drawn to reading from the Book of Hosea. She resisted thinking, ''Lord, I don't want to read all over again about taking back an adulterous mate.'' But the Lord persisted. When she couldn't get away from the inner promptings, she turned to Hosea. Even though this message was given to Israel, God used it to melt her heart and assure her He was to be her fullfillment. ''I am now going to allure her; I will lead her into the desert and speak tenderly to her. There I will give her back her vineyards . . . There she will sing as in the days of her youth . . . 'In that day,' declares the Lord, 'You will call Me ''my husband,'' ' you will no longer call Me 'my master' '' (Hosea 2:14-16).

Yes, Jesus wanted to be Sarah's spiritual husband filling all the voids in her life just as He had with Elaine. Our relationship with Jesus can be compared to a physical relationship with another person—it grows as we interact with each other. By learning to relate to Jesus on an inner level the same way that we relate to others on a physical level, we allow Him to fulfill His role as spiritual husband and give us the lasting and satisfying fulfillment which is possible no other way. Elaine still has times when the pangs of loneliness haunt her and she longs for her husband's presence. But as she concentrates more and more on developing her spiritual relationship with Jesus, this loneliness comes less and less.

Ever since the fall of man we have believed fulfillment would come by catering to and stimulating our physical senses. In reality the opposite is true. Fulfillment does not come by trying to get it. When the Lord becomes our focus and not ourselves, then fulfillment will be ours.

His Character Our Stability

The key to our stability, security, and peace is to always let our fellowship with our Lord, and our responses to life situations and other people rest on His character based on His attributes. Just as a door rests on the strength of its hinges, so do we rest and rely on our God's character. This will mean reprogramming our minds as to who God really is and not replaying the false recordings in our minds made by the sinful nature that taught us to distrust and fear Him. With each situation we learn to respond in view of His character not the way things seem to us.

My sister Jan has coined a phrase "sitting under His character" till all problems melt away. This is quite appropriate in view of the decorative wall hanging she's designed and made which displays the attributes of God. Just under the arrangement she put a small seat where one can literally sit and meditate on his situation in light of God's character till all is well within.

One day Chelle, her oldest daughter, came in very disturbed that her strong desire for owning a horse would never be realized. After showering her with loving understanding, Jan invited Chelle to take the seat under God's character. Since she had been well-taught, Chelle was able to relate her problem to each facet of God's character till she had peace. She reasoned:

1. My God is sovereign. That means He is in control. "For God is the King of all the earth" (Ps. 47:7). Since He is in control, what is happening is for my good and I accept it from Him.

2. My God is righteous—He always does everything right. "The Lord is righteous in all His ways and loving toward all He has made" (145:17).

3. My God is just. "He is the Rock, His works are perfect, and His ways are just" (Deut. 32:4). What is happening to me is fair.

4. My God is immutable. He will never change from being a good God. "I the Lord do not change" (Mal. 3:6).

5. My God is love. He cannot keep from loving me all the time. "And so we know and rely on the love God has for us. God is love" (1 John 4:16).

6. My God is eternal life. "I give them eternal life, and they shall never perish" (John 10:28). I can enjoy His life as long as I don't let

unconfessed sin block that joy. Therefore, Lord, I don't resent what is happening.

7. My God is omnipresent. He is everywhere—even here caring for me. "The eyes of the Lord are everywhere" (Prov. 15:3).

8. My God is omniscient—He knows everything, including what is best for me. "Lord, You know all things" (John 21:17).

9. My God is omnipotent. His power, ability, and authority are without limit. "Great is our Lord and mighty in power" (Ps. 147:5).

10. Then finally the list in the display ends with *God is truth*. He will always keep His promises to me. "Jesus answered, 'I am . . . truth'" (John 14:6). Of course this list isn't exhaustive, but it is a good starting place in identifying with our God and getting to know Him.[1]

Focusing on His character and responding accordingly gives us peace, security, and stability. When my life was so drastically rearranged in 1976, clinging to God and trusting Him was what sustained me. The truths God taught me about being my husband's helpmate had so revolutionized our marriage that DeWitt encouraged me to develop a course around those principles and teach them semiannually in Atlanta. From this came the book, *You Can Be the Wife of a Happy Husband* (Victor), which had also been DeWitt's suggestion.

When requests started coming for seminars in other places, I resisted. My policy had always been that ministering to others could take place only when my role as wife and mother wasn't threatened. Therefore, all teaching had been done during the day while DeWitt was at work and the boys at school. However, DeWitt convinced me that occasional out of town teaching would be good for everyone.

What a joy it was for me to talk about Jesus and see others' needs met. After many, many months of ministering in this way I began to notice DeWitt's response changing from, "We'll get along just fine without you," to "Is it that time once again?" His fading enthusiasm, along with the physical strain my body was showing and the time I had to spend away from our children told me it was time to draw my teaching ministry to a halt.

Teaching was such a joy to me that to stop was like asking me to quit breathing. Not only was it a personal battle, but I considered all the marriages that were falling apart and I knew I could direct troubled couples to the solution. However, I knew God leads through the husband and it was time to redirect my life.

You should know that DeWitt never told me to stop teaching. He wanted me to be happy and would never have dictated to me. Sometimes I have felt it would be easier if he would, then I would not have to observe so closely to see what his actions and attitudes were telling me. But above it all, I knew my God was in control. So even though it looked like the ministry He had given me would fold, I could rest on God and say, "I have set the Lord always before me. Because He is at my right hand, I will not be shaken" (Ps. 16:8).

Once the seminar material was made accessible to others by way of videotapes, slides, cassette tapes along with study helps, I sat back to see what would happen. For awhile it looked like it would all be for nothing. Then God began raising up women all over the country to teach these truths. The demand for seminar materials eventually became so great that I had to allow someone else to manage the distribution.

In retrospect I see that this was the only way God could expand the ministry and enable me to *be* what I was teaching. *Understanding came only after I obeyed.* Now I am convinced I am not to spend my time trying to find out *what* God is doing. I am to spend my time finding out *who* He is and knowing Him. Then I can simply trust Him and rest in His care.

Knowing Him Produces Good Self-Image

Knowing and fellowshipping with God is the basis for a healthy self-image. Self-esteem and self-worth resulting in a healthy self-image will be in direct proportion to our beholding and knowing God in whose image we are created. We do not achieve a good self-image by launching a self-improvement program, then comparing ourselves with others to determine our progress. God says this is foolish. (See 2 Cor. 10:12.)

Allow your interaction with others to draw you closer to Jesus and stabilize your self-image by seeing yourself in light of your relationship with Him, not others. Let's say you and your husband have just had a quarrel. You ask his forgiveness and he says he has forgiven you, but the "icy" treatment continues.

Since you have done all you can, do not be occupied with his response. Instead feed on the fact that Jesus forgives and forgets the moment you confess your sin. Revel in the truth that He never puts you on probation and His love never diminishes regardless of your actions. Let His love and acceptance of you fill the void left by your earthly companion's immaturity. By turning to Jesus in this way He becomes dearer to you, your self-image is strengthened, and you can respond to your husband with the same unconditional love and acceptance Jesus gives you.

My inability to sing well is now a joke between DeWitt and me, but it was not always so. Years ago when he would allude to my "off-key" singing, my heart would be sorely pricked. I wanted to express my joy and tried so hard to sing along with everyone else. It hurt to be reminded how I had failed.

Gradually, I was able to joke about it saying, "God gave you a good voice to drown me out, so I'll sing within your shadow." But now I've stopped pretending and simply rejoice that God gave me the voice I have. I remember that my singing is to Him and it is melodious in His ears! I *do* try to adjust my volume so that others won't be distracted in their worship.

Looking back, I can see that God used DeWitt's unintentional jabs to liberate me in this minor area and strengthen my self-image. There is such freedom when our self-images come from God. If we base our worth on what others think of us, our self-esteem is never on steady ground. But God does not change.

Sarah realized that knowing the One in whose image she was created and seeing herself from God's perspective was the only cure for her badly damaged self-image. For years her self-worth had been built on the fact that she was part of her husband's business and contributed to his financial success. Now she was not only out of his business, but he had chosen another woman with whom to spend part of his time. Perhaps there is no greater humiliation a wife can experience than this. Great was the day Sarah called sharing, "I am more priceless than the most valuable jewels to my Lord. I am the next of kin to God Himself—His child, a member of His forever family. Who I am is not touched by my husband's foolish choices. If he does not know a jewel when he sees it, that is his problem not mine!"

Spend time occupied with knowing God—walking and talking with Him as a way of life—and your self-image will take care of itself. As you get to know the one in whose image you are created, you will get to know yourself. As you learn to see yourself "in Him," your insecurities, unhealthy inadequacies, and apprehensions melt away. You stop pretending or trying to impress others. He is the issue, not you!

Notes

Approximately three months after Chelle obtained peace in her soul concerning whether she would ever own a horse, God gave her one. Numerous circumstances were brought about to accomplish this. The family moved to a rural area giving the necessary space for a horse. The perfect horse was found through an ad in the paper in which the owner had waited for a buyer who would provide a good home. Then at the last minute a saddle was provided through a garage sale. God delights in giving back to us what we lay at His feet!

5
Beholding Him Through His Word

Have you ever thought, "I wish there was something tangible that I could touch or see as proof that I am God's child or that I am in His will? If I just had a postcard from God or something that I could latch on to as visible security, I would feel so much better."

Tangible Security

The need for tangible security began early in my life. Sometime after receiving Christ as my Saviour, I heard others' testimonies of what happened when they became Christians. The assurance I had known began to fade because I had not felt or experienced many of the things they described. Doubts came tumbling in—was I really a Christian? How could I know for sure?

God graciously gave me a pastor who pointed me to God's tangible guidance that would never ever fail me—His Word, the Bible. I read, "Yet to all who received Him, to those who believed in His name, He gave the right to become children of God" (John 1:12).

Then he assured me, "Darien, if you have received Him, then stand on this verse alone as your assurance that you are a child of God. Feelings and experiences vary. They come and go. You can never base anything on them. But you can always trust God's holy Word."

After that, any time doubts came seeking an audience I quoted God's Word and added, "I choose to believe what God says rather than trust my feelings or doubts. I may not feel like God's child today or I may not feel spiritual. But what God says I believe and will move forward with as much assurance as if I felt it.''

Years later I heard a story that served to reinforce my lesson. An old man lay on his deathbed while an angel and the devil battled over the man's eternal fate. The man insisted he was a Christian. When asked for proof he replied describing his time of conversion, ''I had this wonderful experience,'' then he told about it in great detail. When he had finished the devil said, ''I gave you that.'' The angel had to concede that was possible and not permissible proof. Next, the man described a vision he had had, to which the devil came back with the same answer. Finally, the man said, ''For God so loved the world that He gave His one and only Son, that whoever believes in Him shall not perish but have eternal life'' (John 3:16). ''I have believed in Him!'' The matter was settled, and the angel took him on to heaven. The devil could not counterfeit God's Word.

What a comfort to know that God honors His Word above all else. ''You have exalted above all else Your name and Your Word, and You have magnified Your Word above all Your name!'' (Ps. 138:2, AMP) Not only does God honor His Word, but of all the tangible things we can see, only it and people will last forever. ''All men are like grass, and all their glory is like the flowers of the field; the grass withers and the flowers fall, but the Word of the Lord stands forever'' (1 Peter 1:24-25). God's comfort will be ours when we replace insecure feelings with His everlasting Word.

God's Word is not only our tangible security for salvation, but for specific direction in life decisions. When I saw my marriage was in trouble, I turned to His Word. Then I began to see God's plan for me as a wife. It was quite obvious His ways were not my ways.

I remember rising early one morning to seek God's will for a decision I had to make. While pouring my heart out to God asking Him to show me what I should do, He gently reminded me. ''Darien, I never contradict My Word. I have clearly stated that you are to obey your husband. (See Eph. 5:24; 1 Peter 3:1-2.) DeWitt let you know last night that he did not want you to do what you are asking Me to let you do. Remember, I direct your earthly activities through your husband so as to protect you. You had My answer when he spoke.''

I learned that morning that I was not to pray about the things God had clearly spoken about in His Word. I was to simply obey Him. Peace comes from obeying God based on His Word. The responsibility is then His to make it work out for the good of all concerned. "Great peace have they who love Your law; nothing shall offend them or make them stumble" (Ps. 119:165, AMP).

So much heartache can be avoided by searching God's Word till an answer is found rather than acting on what seems right to us. Remember Proverbs 16:25 reminds us how fatal this path can be. "There is a way that seems right to a man but in the end it leads to death."

Judy had just come to know the Lord in an intimate way. She was exuberantly sharing with everyone. The only problem was her husband. Not only did he not share her enthusiasm, but he was totally turned off by her verbal excitement. About this time Judy's ex-fiancé, Jack, just happened on the scene after many years. Judy found an immediate warmth and understanding with Jack that she wasn't getting from her husband. She readily concluded that God had saved him for her.

Within an incredibly short time, Judy divorced her husband and married Jack. Within a year or so, she and Jack were also divorced. Had Judy known and obeyed God's Word, she would not have divorced her husband, but would have sought to relate to him so as to have won him to the Lord through her actions. (See 1 Peter 3:1-2.)

For many of life's decisions, specific Bible verses give clear guidance. In Judy's case she should have been familiar with 1 Corinthians 7:10-11, 13-14, 20; Ephesians 5:20-33; and 1 Peter 3:1-2. There are other specific commands, like *do not commit adultery, do not murder, do not steal*, and so forth. (See Ex. 20:1-17; Prov. 6:16-19; Eph. 4:22-32.)

When specific verses cannot be found, principles drawn from biblical study enable us to reach the right decision. Let's take a very frivolous example, such as trying to decide whether or not to go window shopping. Now there is not a Bible verse that says I should or shouldn't go window shopping. But I can use principles set up in the Word to work out an answer. Remembering God leads me through my husband I consider: would he want me to go? Would I be neglecting responsibilities at home, for the children, or my husband by going? Could we afford to buy anything should I find something I want or like? If not, would I simply be stirring up discontent within my soul? If these check out and I want to go, I would.

In this example, general truths drawn from Scripture were acted upon. They set forth the fact that the married woman's earthly priority is her husband. Next come her children, personal care, household responsibilities, and last her outside activities. She is also considering the wise use of money according to the family budget and her own level of temptation.

One might panic thinking, "I don't know the Bible that well. I'm afraid I will 'blow it.'" This should be an incentive for regularly studying the Word because we know this is the way to have clear guidance. However, we must not be discouraged by all we don't know. We should obey what we do know with an open heart to God as we habitually study His Word, and He will direct us.

God often guides by having us go to people who know the Scriptures, seeking their counsel in areas we aren't sure about. "Plans fail for lack of counsel, but with many advisers they succeed" (Prov. 15:22). God loves to use us in each others' lives. By doing so we "carry each others' burdens, and in this way you will fulfill the law of Christ" (Gal. 6:2).

God's Word Our Bread

In the fall of 1977, a little more than one year after I stopped teaching the marriage seminar and had adjusted to a quieter lifestyle, I realized that I was empty spiritually. I knew everything I had taught was truth and would always be a vital part of my life, but somehow it was no longer enough. The nourishment was gone. I needed new meat. (Incidentally, spiritual malnutrition is one of the hazards of ministering to others. Christian leaders should be careful to take in spiritual food to the same or greater degree than they give it out.)

Deep within me I knew God's Word was the answer. Hadn't Jesus said, "Man does not live on bread alone, but on every word that comes from the mouth of God"? (Matt. 4:4) I felt like I was drowning, yet God's Word became my lifeline.

Somehow I knew I was so low that I had to have an outlined plan to get me going toward spiritual health again. A representative from Bible Memory Association gave me an adult book which outlined specific verses to memorize and meditate on according to the various stages of Christian growth. With eager anticipation I woke each morning looking forward to the spiritual meal Jesus would serve me that day. While working in the kitchen, the book rested over the kitchen sink. While driving in the car, it rode on the dash. Every minute my mind was not occupied with a recipe or watching out at an intersection, I quoted and thought about the verse.

Exciting things began to happen. As I chewed on the written Word, the Spirit caused it to become the living Word within, adding flesh to my spiritually undernourished body. For awhile I held on to the Word because I knew it was my life support. Then I continued to hold on because it was my joy, my nourishment, and my fulfillment. Wasn't that what Jeremiah 15:16 was describing? "When Your words came, I ate them; they were my joy and my heart's delight, for I bear Your name, O Lord God Almighty."

During these times of eating the Word with such great furor, God began opening the eyes of my heart to truths only His Spirit could reveal. An astute teacher can methodically dissect a verse. Such study definitely has its place. But only the Spirit of God can make a verse come alive and reveal its true meaning in a life-changing way. That's the reason Paul tells us to pray for such a revelation. "I keep asking that the God of our Lord Jesus Christ, the glorious Father, may give you the Spirit of wisdom and revelation, so that you may know Him better" (Eph. 1:17).

Driving in the car one particular day while I was quoting Psalm 40:2, God began showing me what He had really done for me as His child. "He brought me up also out of an horrible pit, out of the miry clay, and set my feet upon a rock" (KJV). My heart melted in humble worship before God as I caught the impact of His work on the cross for me. I had done nothing to bring it all about. There was nothing that I could do now. He had done it all!

My Lord showed me I must also act on what He pointed out in His Word. For weeks I wrestled with Psalm 141:3-4. "Set a guard over my mouth, O Lord, keep watch over the door of my lips. Let not my heart be drawn to what is evil, . . . let me not eat of their delicacies."

It is natural for me to speak first and think later. I had felt more at home with a critical tongue than with a praising, thankful vocabulary.

God pricked deep into my heart that day, letting me see the evilness still in my flesh. For days I lay before the Lord, inwardly, helplessly trusting Him to remind me to turn to Him before the wrong thing escaped my mouth. I wanted His nature to pour forth rather than my flesh. Gradually He let me move on to other verses, but I still go back to this one very often for a refresher course!

From experience I began to know the reality of Jesus' words in John 6:35. "I am the bread of life. He who comes to Me will never go hungry." And He says to each of us, "Come to Me, all you who are weary and burdened, and I will give you rest" (Matt. 11:28).

Word Eliminates Idolatry

God's Word enables us to behold Him as He really is. It is so easy to erect a false image of God in our minds and bow down before it, unaware that idolatry is being committed. From childhood experiences or through church training an idea of what God is like is formed in the mind. But our ideas about what God is like must never be set forth by anything which the eye beholds or the hand touches, or anything which exists in sculpture and painting. God warns against this: "I am the Lord your God . . . you shall have no other gods before Me. You shall not make for yourself an idol in the form of anything in heaven or on the earth beneath or in the waters below. You shall not bow down or worship them; for I, the Lord your God, am a jealous God" (Ex. 20:1-5).

In order to eliminate the possibility of having a false image of God in our minds, we should think of Him in terms of the Word's description. "God is light. . . . God is love" (1 John 1:5; 4:16). " 'I am Alpha and Omega, the beginning and the ending,' saith the Lord" (Rev. 1:8, KJV). (Also see Joel 2:13; Pss. 25:8; 103:3; John 4:24; 1 Cor. 1:9.)

Even though we cannot see God face to face (Ex. 33:20), He has revealed Himself in His Son. "He is the exact likeness of the unseen God—the visible representation of the invisible" (Col. 1:15, AMP). As we get to know Jesus, we get to know the Father as well. (See John 14:7.)

Above all, we should see God as a Being from whom we are to receive all good. No matter how sinful or unworthy we may feel, we should approach our merciful heavenly Father calmly, peacefully, and fearlessly knowing He loves us completely.

Developing the proper image of God in our minds is crucial in view of the fact that we become like what we worship. "Those who make idols are like them; so is every one who trusts and relies on them" (Ps. 135:18, AMP). As we start replacing wrong concepts about God with what He says about Himself in the Word, we will find a sweeter rapport and fellowship than ever before.

Quiet Time with the Word

A regular time and place to come before the Lord with His Word is necessary. When and where will probably vary according to your needs and those in your family. For a while when our children were young I got up before the rest of the family. Now that the children are older, I usually have my devotional time after everyone is gone for the day.

Many books give guidelines for an effective quiet time with our Lord. Ask Him what He would have you to do. My time varies. Sometimes I use a devotional book combined with the Scripture reading. Other times I either read the Word according to some organized plan or as dictated by my needs. Often, a good inspirational book is combined with my Bible study. Since it is easy for me to try to find security through predetermined plans, I have to be careful not to lock myself into a system that destroys God's lordship in my life.

Spending time in the Word cleanses our minds of the pollution we pick up from the world. Often by spending time in the work force, visiting the neighbors, or counseling others, we are exposed to wrong thinking. Our minds need to be renewed toward godliness. Sitting down with the Word and just reading and reading counteracts the worldly viewpoint and once again puts us on God's wavelength. Jesus said the Word cleansed His disciples and also purifies the church (John 15:3; Eph. 5:26).

Whatever method is used during the devotional time, try reading the Scripture passage out loud. By reading out loud, you get a greater exposure to what the passage is really saying. Not only do you *see* the words, but you *hear* and *say* them. As you listen, drop all your preconceived ideas of what the verse means. Ask God to enlighten the eyes of your heart so that you will hear what He is saying to you.

As you are reading out loud ask yourself the following questions to be sure you are getting what is being conveyed. *Who was this book written to? Why was it written? What were the conditions at the time in which the people were living? Who said these words? What do the words themselves mean?* Also read whole sections at a time so that a particular verse is not taken out of context and misunderstood. Remember that a principle or concept is never built on one single verse. The truth will be reinforced throughout Scripture.

Should God's written Word seem to contradict itself at times, resolve the conflict in light of His character and His completed work for you on the cross. Refuse to believe anything that contradicts these two basic truths. God will in time remove the contradictions.

After you've answered these questions, paraphrase the passage. Often it helps to write it down. As you do so put your name in the verse, making it personal as God meant it to be.

Often it is exciting to do a word study concerning whatever is on your heart. For instance, if you should be very weary, do a study on the word *labor* using your Bible's concordance, cross references, and other available study aids. Ask God to speak to your heart and He will.

Another precious way to fellowship with Jesus through the Word is to pray the Scriptures back to Him. The idea here is not to cover large portions of Scripture, but to come to Him quietly and humbly letting Him speak to your heart. When a phrase, verse, or verses touch your heart so as to surface the following response, "Oh, I need that, I want to be like that, or that is the way I feel about You Lord," then stop and say it out loud to the Lord.

Other times quietly take a section of Scripture or perhaps only a verse and meditate on it in the following way so as to plunge into the very depths of the words letting God's presence surround you like a sweet aroma. Using the Lord's Prayer to illustrate, one might say, "Our Father." Stop there and let the full meaning of that phrase deeply touch your heart. Believe that the God who lives inside you is indeed willing to be your Father. Pour out your heart to Him as a weak helpless child pours out his heart to his father. *Never* doubt your Lord's deep love for you. *Never* doubt His desire to hear you. Call His

Name. Utter a word of love to Him. Wait for awhile in silence then continue on in the Lord's Prayer.

As you speak the words, "Thy kingdom come," call upon your Lord, the King of Glory, to reign in you. Give yourself up to God, so that He may do in your heart what you have so long been a failure in trying to do. Acknowledge before Him His right to rule over you. Periodically wait in silence before Him.

Next, praying the words, "Your will be done on earth as it is in heaven," humble yourself before God. Earnestly ask Him to accomplish His whole will in you and through you. Surrender your heart into His hands. Surrender your freedom into His hands. Yield to your Lord His right to do with you as He pleases. Since His will is for His children to love Him, utter words of love and praise to Him. The Song of Solomon is a wonderful book to use to respond to the Lord with words of love. Begin with: 1:3; 2:10, 16.

Regardless of how you spend your quiet time, keep in mind that the whole purpose is to behold God as well as to have bread for the day's nourishment. If you have to miss this time don't panic, feel guilty, or condemned. Simply turn to Him fellowshipping with Him as you go through the day in light of truths and lessons that He's personally dealing with you on or that are precious to you.

Obedience to the Living Word

As we allow God's living Word, the Lord Jesus Christ, to make the written Word alive to us, we begin to enjoy a sweet precious fellowship with Him. His life becomes our life. "God, who *has called you into fellowship with His Son Jesus Christ our Lord,* is faithful" (1 Cor. 1:9).

Each heart yearns for a oneness in fellowship with the Lord as Jesus described having with the Father. "Whatever I say is just what the Father has told Me to say" (John 12:50). In striving for this oneness, we must realize that we have interferences of self or the flesh and sin to overcome. Yet being sensitive to the leading of His Spirit is to be a real part of our lives (John 10:30).

Each person must observe how God uniquely deals with and leads him. Various descriptions of God's inner leading are given by New Testament believers. (See Acts 11:12; 16:7; 17:16; Rom. 8:14, 16;

1 Cor. 2:10; 1 Peter 3:18; 1 John 5:7-8.) Terminology today varies all the way from *inner prompting, being led, inner voice, still small voice,* and *prompting of my spirit by His Spirit* to the more extreme *Jesus told me to* or *God said.* These bolder expressions can be offensive to more conservative Christians. Some people think that believers who use bold phrases like this are trying to make Christianity a weird mystical experience. But when we look at the meanings behind the phrases, we see that the bolder phrases convey the same truths that the other phrases do—only in different words.

Guidelines to Eliminate Error

In developing an attentive ear to our Lord's inner leading, these guidelines should help remove confusion and error.

First and foremost, having the living Word witness to our hearts necessitates being full of the written Word, since God does not operate apart from His revealed Word. His inner guidance is always consistent with the written Word. And His written Word will always support, confirm, and uphold what He is directing us to do. Thus the Scriptures are always our first checkpoint in knowing His leading.

Next, to respond to His prompting, we must be attentive to Him. "In *returning to Me* and *resting in Me* you shall be saved" (Isa. 30:15, AMP), reminds us to be available to Him with a sensitive listening spirit.

Thirdly, Jesus must be Lord of our lives. We must be willing to do what He directs, even if it is opposed to what we prefer. He will not give direction to unyielded hearts.

When we ask Jesus to be Lord in our lives, it means that we immediately deal with any sin as He exposes it to us. Not doing so grieves God's Spirit within and thus His guidance. (See Eph. 4:30.)

Fourthly, His guidance will be accompanied by peace. "And let the peace [soul harmony which comes] from the Christ rule [act as umpire continually] in your hearts—deciding and settling with finality all questions that arise in your minds" (Col. 3:15, AMP).

An incident with Lisa illustrates the application of these third and fourth principles. Following a lead given to me by a friend, I met Lisa who agreed to do some professional art work for a project on which I was working. I left my crude sketches, explaining that she did not have to do the lettering if she did not want to—we could use typesetting if necessary. I added that we were debating on whether to use green or blue as the background color.

Twenty-four hours later I stood in her kitchen viewing a cover that thrilled my soul. I asked Lisa to share with me why she had chosen to do the lettering and why she had so boldly stated that the color was to be green. She explained that as she viewed the project and considered the color green, she immediately thought *Yuk!* From deep within her being she became aware of an uneasiness. Then she thought, *Who said yuk, You or me?* Immediately she realized she had made a judgment based on her past training and knowledge (which can so easily puff up). She agreed not to reject or accept the color green, but relinquish that decision to Jesus.

After drawing the pictures, she took out her lettering book. When she tried out the third type of lettering, a peaceful assurance let her know this was the one to use. The matter was settled.

Once the cover was finished she tried to visualize the different colors on it. An excitement surrounded by peace welled up from deep within over the thought of a green color. Needless to say, the finished cover was much more pleasing than what I'd hoped for.

Fifthly, God's leading will be consistent with what He is saying to others. Confirmation is often needed to settle God's guidance in our inner being. When DeWitt told me that His Way Library should be managed by someone else because it was becoming too much for me, I thought, *Who on earth would want to do it?* Immediately, I said within to Jesus, "Lord, show me who You have in mind. I know You have someone or You would not be directing this way through my husband."

There was no immediate answer. Later as I was going about my routine chores, the thought burst forth, *Haralson Printing. It would be perfect to coordinate His Way Library with their Christian printing business*. It fit! It made sense. I felt sure it was God's leading.

Next morning I called the owners. I did not tell them that God had chosen them to do this (even though I did feel so). I simply presented the idea. A few days later they excitedly agreed, and I knew for sure God had directed me to ask them.

Sixthly, God's leading is always consistent with Christ's finished work on the cross. We can take no credit in obtaining our salvation or maintaining our walk with Him (Eph. 2:8-9). Any prompting that implies we are more spiritual or holy by something we do is not God's leading. Christ imputes His righteousness to us and infuses His holiness to us as we walk with Him.

Seventhly, God's direction is always consistent with His character based on His attributes. This should eliminate any fear or distrust of Him. Keep in mind that maturity plays a significant role in recognizing our Lord's leading. Notice Jesus speaks of His sheep, not His lambs, hearing His voice (John 10:4). When we first become Christians, we are brand new people inside. But we must grow up into maturity on the inside, just as our physical bodies do on the outside. Do not misunderstand. A new Christian *can* hear and obey God's voice. But it is with maturity that this is strengthened. Since our functioning process was reversed because of sin, we have to learn not to listen to our flesh, the old programming in our minds, or the enemy. The following checklist should help in distinguishing the different inner voices.

Checklist for Different Inner Leadings

The flesh very subtly leads us into self-pity, pride, defeatism, and self-condemnation. This is characterized by a "poor ole me" or "I'm a failure" attitude. The flesh also seeks to exert itself and is bossy and forceful. It calls attention to self, not Christ. To determine if this is the case, we should ask ourselves why we are doing what we are.

Our enemy, Satan, is an accuser. He attacks God's character, saying that God does not love us, He is not fair, or He is trying to make us miserable. Satan seeks to depress, torment, and destroy us. He is the author of all sinful fear. (See John 8:44; Rev. 12:10; Job 1:6-11; 1 Peter 5:7-9.) Satan also attempts to use pressure to drive us into taking situations into our own hands.

Satan causes us to doubt ourselves, God's Word, and fellow Christians. His influence seeks to put us in bondage. If anything in our walk with the Lord is putting us in bondage rather than giving liberty, we should back off and reexamine the Word (2 Cor. 2:17).

While Satan accuses and condemns, God convicts. With His conviction comes a knowledge of what we did wrong and a realization that we can have forgiveness, based on Christ's work on the cross. With condemnation comes an air of confusion, vagueness, and frustration. But God's inner working of conviction is clear and specific.

However, if what we feel God is saying to us is also what we would naturally like to do, we should WAIT! We must give our natural desires time to subside should our leading not be of the Lord. Our Lord does not push, even though He is persistent. Yet we can resist so long that we harden our hearts against God's leading.

Our Lord's leading is gentle, kind, comforting, and clear. However, His guidance may not be completely clear exactly when we want it to be. Many times in my life His leading could be described as a *growing knowing*. At first only a glimpse of a truth or what He'd have me to do is grasped. As He is continually sought for understanding and guidance, clarity eventually comes forth so that I can say, "Now I know. It fits! There is confirmation in my inner being."

Even our Lord's harsh words to us are accompanied by gentleness. What may seem stern to us is done with utmost tenderness. If we never hear our Lord speak harshly, we may not be listening to Him. For a year or two I occasionally wondered before the Lord why I didn't seem to reap as many astounding insights from a simple reading of the Word as my sister did. Mine seemed to spring more from fellow Christians' teachings based on the Word. Often I felt guilty, thinking there was something wrong with me or that my insights were second hand and therefore not as spiritual.

I will never forget the morning as I was making our bed thinking through this once again. Suddenly this thought came to me: "Darien, if I dealt with you like I do Jan, you would be prideful! I must do as I am doing so you cannot take any credit." I knew that thought did not come from me! I was totally surprised. But with the realization came a peace and confirmation that it was from my Lord and that He was right. I was then content with His ways because I knew they were best for me.

Should God's leading produce opposite results than anticipated, we shouldn't conclude that the leading was not from God. Helen made that mistake. She had just become aware of God's desire to direct her and felt certain He was telling her to speak to her pastor to stop at her husband's job and witness to him. Her pastor abruptly scolded her for trying to be God in her husband's life. (If you didn't know Helen, you might think her pastor was uncompassionate. However, Helen was a very manipulating woman who had indeed been trying to play God in her mate's life.)

Helen concluded, because her pastor's response was so painful to her, that this business of following God's inner leading was ridiculous. After all, look what happened to her when she obeyed. But in reality her pastor's response *was* God's leading. The Lord was trying to teach her a very valuable lesson. What more appropriate tool could He have used than her pastor?

A Natural Relaxed Walk

Does God regularly prompt us with specific directions and insights for each detail of the day as we relate to Him? Reading through the Book of Acts, we see that the apostles moved *by faith doing the obvious* unless God intervened giving specific direction or stopped them otherwise (Acts 16:1-13).

When we are yielded to the Lord, we can trust by faith that doing the obvious or following our innermost desires when all of these checkpoints are met is God's leading for us. We don't wait for specific directions, but are always open to His intervention. In my own life, the more distinct insights seem to come either as a bonus or in accordance with my needs.

Above all we should not be threatened by others' testimonies of how God deals with them. We must not try to get God to duplicate in our lives what He does in another's life. Remember Jesus dealt differently with the disciples, and He will with us also. He allowed only three of the twelve disciples to witness His magnificent transfiguration. These three had a more dramatic experience with the Lord than the others, but were loved no more. His plan for their lives was simply different.

Our job is to behold God in light of His Word, giving Him complete freedom to deal with us as He sees best. In turn we praise Him for His guidance which gives Him the glory He is due. As we walk with Him as a way of life, His leading will not be characterized by the traumatic or dramatic. But our fellowship with Him will become so natural that we will often not be aware that it is supernatural.

6
Beholding
Him Through Choice

"I'm acting just like my six-month-old, Mark," Sarah laughed. "Just this morning as I changed his messy diaper, he wiggled, squirmed, and resisted my every effort to clean him up. Of course, that didn't keep me from changing him, it only made it harder and longer. Isn't that the way it is with us and the Lord? He is delivering us out of the mess sin has caused in us. The longer we resist choosing His will just makes it harder on us."

Sarah was right. When we become God's children, our Father is committed to restoring us to the likeness of His Son. "Being confident of this, that He who began a good work in you will carry it on to completion until the day of Christ Jesus" (Phil. 1:6). As we commit our wills to His will, the needed changes in our lives are brought about with greater ease.

Will—Key Element
The will, which is the controlling element of the soul, is the key to the ease with which our spiritual progress comes about. Other people, circumstances, or demonic forces are not what determines the course we take, but our wills. When we deliberately choose God's will, our direction is set. The more we choose His will, the easier it becomes. Uniting our wills to His will brings peace, contentment, and overflowing joy.

When we keep in mind what life is all about, choosing His will is easier. Our purpose in life is to display the very life of our Lord in a dependent love relationship. He is to be our God rather than our trying to be as or like God. He is to be exalted and lifted up, not ourselves. Jesus confirms that He was committed to the Father's will for Him, not His own (John 5:30; 6:38). For Christ, doing God's will was the source of soul-satisfying nourishment. "My food is to do the will of Him who sent Me and to finish His work" (4:34).

Willing His Will

"I want God's will in my life" is the genuine, deep down response of each of God's children. But often we think we're choosing His will when we really aren't. So subtle and gradual is the take over of our will as opposed to the deliberate submitting to His will. One way God exposes this is by using people and circumstances to keep us from being deceived as to whose will we are choosing.

For years DeWitt and I dreamed of moving to the country on a small plot of land. However, we'd agreed this wouldn't be practical till at least one or two of our three sons were gone from home, lessening our financial responsibilities as well as eliminating the need for as big a home. So imagine my shock when I arrived home late in November after a week's stay in Florida to learn DeWitt had been looking for our country home!

I knew the principle of submission and that God's will is known through one's husband. I would have counseled any woman to lovingly embrace her husband's plans and tactfully share any reservations she had with him. However, believing a truth and applying it are two different things. Rather than relaxing and thanking God that He was in control, it was as if my heels dug into the car's floor trying to bring things under my control.

I did respond as I should have with, "Honey, that is exciting. Fill me in on all the details." But he had hardly finished the details when I revealed my mounting unrest with, "Have you prayed about this? Then please promise me you will pray once again just to be sure!"

My will was in full swing even though it was not obvious to me. All my thinking was very logical and reasonable, I felt. Yet nothing made sense. Who shops for a home in November or December? Any real estate person would agree the prospects weren't good then. We had one son in college and the other two fast approaching. Interest rates were going sky high and inflation was at an all-time high. Who in their right mind would consider tripling house notes?

Such questions were not wrong to have and to lovingly work through with my husband. My problem was my unteachable spirit—inwardly I *insisted* my way was right. God used my mate to expose my willfulness through this new set of circumstances. Once God made me aware of this, the situation became critical. Would I deliberately choose God's will and disregard my feelings and logical reasoning—or insist on my way?

Through this incident God taught me afresh that the first step in beholding Him through choice is to *will His will*. We choose submission or resignation to Him, then the emotions and understanding follow. But we do not start with feelings or logical reasoning. Often according to the severity of the situation, we may need to say to ourselves as many as 100 times a day: "I will Thy will."

Once this step is taken, it's exciting to see the second step come about. *We are choosing His will*. As we continue to say, as often as necessary, "I choose Thy will," another change will become evident. *We then begin delighting in His will*.

In summary, once God shows us that our will is not resigned to His will, we should deliberately turn away from self-will to His will. We begin by willing it, we come to choose, and we end by delighting in it. Therein is the secret of beholding God through choice.

God often uses others to force us to choose His will. One morning when the phone rang and I recognized Sarah's voice, I thought, *Oh no! I need someone to hold up Christ to me today rather than trying to help another behold Him. I'm so down emotionally and spiritually I'll never help her*.

However, by faith I told her what I *knew* was true—rather than what I *felt* at the time. When we finished she was beholding God and thanking me for turning her eyes to Him. I shared, "Sarah, God has used you to help me as much as I have helped you today. I was about ready to fall apart myself when you called."

Then, she gave me a jolt when she responded, "You always seem to have it all together. I never thought you would ever experience the rotten things I do."

I was amazed anyone would view me that way and assured her there are no superhumans. Each of us works through initally the same things and all find victory the same way—by beholding God.

Willing to Be Willing

"How can I deliberately choose God's will when I'm not sure I want His will?" was Becky's question as we talked at my kitchen table. When I asked if she was willing to be willing, she said, "Yes!" Without realizing it, Becky had embraced God's will simply by being willing to be willing. David's cry in Psalm 51:12 was similar to Becky's response. "Restore to me the joy of Your salvation and grant me a willing spirit, to sustain me."

Becky went home that day willing to be willing. She demonstrated her willingness by saying and doing the things she knew God would have her to do. Before long, she was embracing and delighting in God's will.

"I am willing to choose His will now, but how can I be sure I will if times should get ever more painful?" This is a question with which many of us have struggled. Eliminate that doubt right now by committing to Him that which you fear you might not be able to commit in the future. The following is what a young woman by the name of Much-Afraid in Hannah Hurnard's allegory, *Hinds' Feet on High Places*,[1] stated in anticipation of upcoming pain while laying her all on the altar before her Lord. "I am a very great coward. I am afraid that the pain may cause me to try to resist You. Will You bind me to the altar in some way so that I cannot move? I would not like to be found struggling while the will of my Lord is done."

Our comfort against our fears is answered in 1 Thessalonians 5:24. "The One who calls you is faithful and He will do it." Read Ephesians 1:13-14 and Philippians 1:6 for added comfort.

No Guilt over Emotions

As I confessed my willfulness to God and deliberately embraced His will as revealed through my husband, house-hunting became exciting. As I praised Him for exposing my willful spirit I added, "Lord, allow each and every detail of this move to happen in such a way that only You can be the explanation." God honored my prayer. Within weeks I learned how varied are His marvelous ways of working.

After only three short weeks of very limited looking, we found the place that suited each family member's needs. Within three days during the second week of December when no one buys houses, we had a contract on our house as a result of simply putting a sign in the yard. Details were falling in place so quickly and smoothly it could only be explained as our Lord's doing.

We smoothly sailed through the next six weeks while the different parties applied and qualified for loans. However, when an occasional hint arose that things might not go well, I tried as best I could to keep my "want to ers" in neutral and genuinely said, "Lord, I want to be where You want us whether it is to move or not to move. I will embrace either choice with equal enthusiasm."

At that time God was teaching me in a deeper sense that His overflowing joy wasn't dependent on people or circumstances. I was learning "to be content whatever the circumstances" (Phil. 4:11). I knew with absolute confidence that this principle was true, however, when the real estate agent would call in the final days before closing saying, "I'm not sure we can pull it off," I found my mood dropping. Then hours later another call would say, "All looks good," and my feelings accelerated. I was deliberately and genuinely choosing God's will, yet I felt frustrated by my fluctuating emotions. My inner battle was compounded by the realization that DeWitt needed my support and positive attitude most during those down times. I felt I was failing him.

My emotions hit bottom the night we were to close the sale and our buyers didn't show up. I couldn't keep the tears from flowing. DeWitt and I knew God was trying to teach us something, but we weren't sure what.

Our buyers showed up the next morning at the final hour. The closing was like sailing rough seas compared to the smooth sailing in the beginning, but God had answered my prayer. All could be explained no other way than that our Lord was at work!

Later, God made it clear what He was saying to me. Feelings are not the issue. Never make them the issue in your mind. The issue is: are you choosing His will to the best of your ability? If so, receive what comes from Him without any guilt. Don't resist, fight, or feel guilty about your emotions. It is all right to feel emotional at times.

Emotions become a liability only when they are your direction givers or when you attempt to use them to get your way, manipulate another, or fall into self-pity. Otherwise, remember that God gave you your emotions and they are designed to be a healthy release.

The distinction between peace, contentment, and overflowing joy and "happy feelings" was clear. Peace and overflowing joy come from beholding God and committing our will to His. Happy feelings may or may not accompany this but whether they do or don't doesn't affect our spirituality.

As we commit our wills to Him beholding Him through the rough spots, we can usually look back seeing what He has been doing. Could that be what the psalmist meant when he said, "Surely goodness and love will *follow me* all the days of my life"? (Ps. 23:6) God's goodness and love are not always recognizable while we are going through a crisis. But later the understanding comes. (See John 13:7.)

Mind Set During Dry Periods

Beholding Him through choice rather than through our emotions keeps us from being deceived during dry periods. When all is going smoothly, you are aware of God's presence, enjoying His gifts and blessings and feeling "spiritual," it is easy to choose His ways and let Him be our God. Often God allows times of dryness, or times when we do not feel His presence or even worse feel He has forsaken us, to strengthen and reaffirm in our own beings who our God is. Is God our God for what we can get from Him or because we are committed to Him? It is easy to cross that fine line without realizing it.

During such times of feeling forsaken, what do we do? We concentrate on what God says about us in the Word rather than what we feel. Colossians 1:27 says, *"Christ in you,* the hope of glory." Not only does Hebrews 13:5 say, *"Never will I leave you; never will I forsake you"* but Galatians 2:20 points out, "I have been crucified with Christ and I no longer live, but *Christ lives in me."* We purposefully concentrate on these truths rather than on our feelings.

God reminds us over and over that our direction comes as a result of a mind set on things above, not on our feelings. "For those who are according to the flesh set their minds on the things of the flesh, but those who are according to the Spirit, the things of the Spirit"

(Romans 8:5, NASB). When Peter was entrapped by Satan, Jesus said to him, "You are not *setting your mind* on God's interest, but man's" (Matt. 16:23, NASB).

Once we have set our mind on things above, we should humbly wait upon God and give Him the freedom to do in our lives as He sees fit.

Times of spiritual dryness are designed for our growth and benefit, giving approval to the next stage of development. An old story of how one Christian dreamed that she saw three others at prayer when the Master drew near, illustrates this point.

As He approached the first of the three, He bent over her in tenderness and grace, with smiles full of radiant love and spoke to her in accents of purest, sweetest music.

Leaving her, He came to the next, but only placed His hand on her bowed head and gave her one look of loving approval.

The third woman He passed almost abruptly, without stopping for a word or glance. In her dream, the woman said to herself, *How greatly He must love the first one, to the second He gave His approval, but none of the special demonstrations of love He gave the first; and the third must have grieved Him deeply for He gave her no word at all and not even a passing look. I wonder what she has done, and why He made so much difference between them?*

Then the Lord said, "O woman! You have wrongly interpreted Me. The first kneeling woman needs all the weight of My tenderness and care to keep her feet in My narrow way. She needs demonstrations of My love every moment of the day. Without it she would fall and fail.

"The second woman has stronger faith and deeper love, and I can trust her to trust Me however things may go and whatever people do.

"The third woman, whom I seemed to neglect, has faith and love of the finest quality. I am training her by quick and drastic processes for the highest and holiest service.

"She is coming to know and trust Me so intimately that she is no longer discouraged by any circumstances. She trusts Me when sense and reason and every finer instinct of the natural heart would rebel. She knows that I am working in her for eternity. She doesn't know the explanation now, but she will understand hereafter.

"Often My love is silent because I love beyond the power of words to express or of the human heart to understand. For your sake you need to learn to love and trust Me in Spirit without anything outward to call it forth."

Dry periods are not times to dread but to re-evaluate if our God is God or if His blessings have become our god. It is a time of discipline whereby we purposely set our minds on things above. Dry periods indicate continued growth and strengthening in our lives leading us to greater degrees of maturity. Thus we can embrace them knowing He is in control.

Work Out Your Salvation

Beholding God through choice means allowing God to use people and circumstances to help "work out our salvation" as Philippians 2:12 states. "Therefore, my dear friends . . . continue to work out your salvation with fear and trembling." Notice this verse does not say work *for* your salvation, it says work *out* your salvation.

When we became Christians we became brand new people on the inside—the people God originally designed us to be. Then the process begins of working out the old person that was crucified with Christ on the cross and manifesting the brand new person. Sometimes the old person is compared to the leaves that die on the trees in the fall when the sap stops flowing. Even though the leaves are dead it takes jolts, winds, and new growth to remove them.

Likewise, God uses people and circumstances to expose our self-ishness, willfulness, and desire to be our own gods. When He does, we should (1) apply His work on the cross to that sin, allowing Him to clean it out as an antiseptic swab cleanses a wound; then (2) turn to Him allowing Him to draw us more intimately to Himself and fill us more with His fullness.

Pain is often associated with releasing our will to God's will and working out our salvation. Not only is this true for us, but it was also true for Jesus. He prayed, " 'Father, if You are willing, take this cup from Me; yet not My will, but Yours be done.' And being in anguish, He prayed more earnestly, and His sweat was like drops of blood falling to the ground" (Luke 22:42, 44).

Elaine is familiar with the pain that can come when we turn loose of our will to embrace God's. Her soul was still raw and tender from the pain of Tom leaving her and marrying another woman. On top of that, her oldest daughter's rebellion was ripping her apart. Karen, the daughter, reasoned, "Dad was a deacon and a Sunday School teacher and he is living an immoral, reckless life—why shouldn't I?" This 18-year-old then quit attending church and was defying her mother's curfews.

One particular night Elaine left a woman's retreat to spend the night at home. She had been struggling with her own feelings, her children's welfare, and Karen's disobedience. As she drove home she recommitted each of them to Jesus. "Lord, they are Yours not mine. Take them and manifest Your glory through them regardless of what it takes!" Elaine meant each word. It was a prayer of relinquishment of the only family she had left—her children.

About midnight the phone rang and Karen said, "Momma, I'll be late." What a surprise. She hadn't called when she was going to be late in months.

About 12:30 the phone rang again and Karen's voice echoed over the line, "I haven't started for home yet, Momma."

For some reason and definitely not out of habit because Karen had previously resented any help or suggestions, Elaine said, "Karen, do you want me to come get you?"

"Would you, Momma?"

"Yes," Elaine responded.

"Well, I really don't know where I am. If I am not home in an hour have the police look for me," Karen said as she hung up.

Elaine could have panicked, but she committed her will and Karen's care to her Lord. She deliberately said, "Lord, through all the pain I have experienced, You have worked out selfishness, independence, sins of all kinds, so that now You are so very near and dear to me. I wouldn't trade that for anything. Less than an hour ago I gave Karen back to You. I trust You to take her through whatever is necessary to work out her rebellion. I trust You because You are fair. You do all things rightly with the greatest compassion and love. I see You as being in control and I praise You for what You are doing."

Then Elaine sat and watched out the window while the minutes ticked by. Shortly before 2 A.M. a car drove up, a door slammed, and

Karen ran up the driveway. Elaine breathed a prayer of praise thanking Jesus that she was all right.

What had Elaine done? She committed her will to God's will regardless of the hurt involved. She did not attempt to act as God by telling Him how to carry out His will, when to carry it out, or under what conditions. She humbly submitted to His will, letting Him be God. Such actions allow His surgery to proceed with the least amount of pain.

In turn God drew Elaine closer to Himself showing her that real life and freedom come only by trusting Him. Now she knows that real love is loving with an open hand. Many times before, Elaine had opened her hands of her children as best she could, but God used the incident that night to pry them open even more fully.

No one loses when we trust our Lord. Not only did Elaine benefit, but that night seemed to be the turning point for Karen. Gradually her rebellion began to die. She started back to church and within a year a young man came to a Bible study she was instrumental in starting. He said, "I came because I wanted to see why you are smiling all the time."

Keeping our hands open before God with regard to our own wills and those of our loved ones is the way we behold God and enjoy others without abusing them. Opening up our hands is easier when we see God's hand outstretched under ours, receiving and encompassing all we release. We know that He, who gave His all for us—His life, would never give to us anything except what is for our good. "No good thing will He withhold from those who walk uprightly" (Ps. 84:11, AMP).

The old story of a monk is a gentle reminder to me when I try to tell God what to do. "I need oil," said the old monk. So he planted an olive sapling. "Lord," he prayed, "it needs rain that its tender roots may drink and swell. Send gentle showers." The Lord sent gentle showers. "Lord," prayed the monk, "my tree needs sun. Send sun, I pray Thee." The sun shone, gilding the dripping clouds. "Now frost, my Lord, to brace its tissues," cried the monk. Behold, the little tree stood sparkling with frost, but at evening it died.

Then the monk sought the cell of a brother monk and told his strange experience. "I, too, planted a little tree," he said. "See, it thrives well. But I entrust my tree to its God. He who made it knows better what it needs than a man like me. I laid no conditions. I fixed not ways nor means. "Lord, send what it needs," I prayed, "storm or sunshine, wind, rain, or frost. Thou hast made it and Thou dost know."

Let's join the second monk, deferring to God's will, and welcome any exposure of willfulness those around us reveal, so that our salvation will be worked out in fear and trembling. As our hearts are regularly lifted up to God saying, "To do Your will, O my God, is my desire" (40:8), we will not become insensitive to His will causing Him to do to us what He had to do to Israel. "So I gave them up to their own hearts' lust and let them go after their own stubborn will, that they might follow their own counsels" (81:12, AMP).

His Will—Dependency

"I want to know and do God's will. How can I know what His will is?" This is a legitimate question asked by many Christians. God's will is that we be completely and helplessly dependent upon Him at all times. He reminds us that "apart from Me you can do nothing" (John 15:5). In this dependent walk with Jesus, He says He will be our light (8:12). That light is usually not a spotlight showing us who, what, where, and when for long distances ahead, but more like a lantern that shows only the next step. He often must do it this way to keep us utterly dependent on Him.

The dependency we are to have upon God could be compared to the dependency a child has upon its mother through the umbilical cord while in the womb. Through this union and dependency the mother's life is in a very real sense the child's life. He lives because she lives. When he kicks his tiny feet, he could say with accuracy, "That was my mommie's work—at least, it was her strength. An extension of her own life." He lives, moves, and has his being with his mother.[2]

Through our birth into God's family, He rejoined us to Himself by way of a "spiritual umbilical cord." We live, move, and have our being in the womb of His protection and care. We must now learn to live in the same total dependency upon Him that the unborn child knows upon its mother in order to enjoy experientially the life Jesus paid for us to have and know.

While on earth, Jesus demonstrated the same complete dependency upon the Father that we are to have upon Him. He said, "I tell you the truth, the Son can do nothing by Himself; He can do only what He sees His Father doing" (John 5:19). Not only did Jesus do only what He saw the Father doing, but He said nothing except what the Father told Him to say (12:49).

Such dependency is to be a way of life. When I first learned to walk in the Spirit, I somehow had the idea that eventually I would arrive at a place of spiritual independence. Then I began to notice that I moved from one situation that kept me helplessly dependent upon Him to another. Now I realize that maturity is not myself getting stronger, but becoming more helplessly dependent upon Him. The Christian life then begins to be easier because we learn to feel at home in our helplessness.

However, the concept of complete dependency on anyone other than ourselves, and this includes God, is diabolically opposed to everything within our flesh. Those with naturally strong talents and self-confidence have a doubly hard job coming to this place of helpless dependency on God. One well trained piano teacher bristled at this idea when she heard John 15:5 quoted. "Apart from Me you can do nothing." She adamantly stated, "What do you mean I can do nothing! I can teach piano quite well all by myself, thank you!"

What she did not realize was that she could do nothing of spiritual worth or lasting value. All the things we do in our own strength will ultimately be burned up, because in God's economy they are as filthy rags. (See 1 Cor. 3:12-15; Isa. 64:6.) We are totally helpless to produce anything of eternal or spiritual value apart from God. That applies to what is accomplished in our own lives as well as the overflow into others' lives.

Dependency Laced with Cooperation

A crucial balance between a helpless dependency upon God and what I must do in cooperation with Him must be maintained. Often only one side is dealt with and problems arise. Even in attempting to point out the intricate equation, I know balance will not be gained apart from understanding from our Lord.

A typical experience in a marital relationship can be used as an illustration. A misunderstanding arises. Ugly, unkind words are exchanged. Unloving actions are exhibited. The Lord convicts you that the fruit of His Spirit is not being manifested. You confess your sin (1 John 1:9) and know you are forgiven based on His work on the cross. Once you are clean before God, you may need to ask forgiveness from your mate if you have offended or hurt him.

Next, Jesus shows you that your actions and words must display love toward your mate. You are to respond to him as if you felt love. That means when you crawl into bed you snuggle up with a hug like always. Yes, that is difficult. But obeying God means that you show love to your mate even when you may not feel like it.

Doing what we know to be right rather than what we feel like doing is called "faithing it" or living by faith. Not "faking it" as one woman misunderstood me to say. It is not hyprocrisy as some may contend. Obedience to God's Word can never be labeled hyprocrisy.

We must remember at all times that it is "in Him we live and move and have our being" (Acts 17:28). Even as we do the necessary cooperating, we do so in helpless dependency knowing only He can bring about the real inward changes in His timing as He sees fit. The verse in my kitchen window keeps me aware of this truth. "My eyes are ever on the Lord, for only He will release my feet from the snare" (Ps. 25:15).

Sweet Fragrance

As we link our will to His will, our lives give off a sweet fragrance to those around us, to the unseen world, and to our precious God. "We have become a spectacle to the world—a show in the world's amphitheatre—with both men and angels [as spectators]" (1 Cor. 4:9, AMP) "But thanks be to God, who always leads us in triumphal procession in Christ and through us spreads everywhere the fragrance of the knowledge of Him. For we are to God the aroma of Christ among those who are being saved and those who are perishing" (2 Cor. 2:14-16).

The burnt offering that the Israelites carried out according to God's instructions was a portrayal of our Lord Jesus Christ's complete surrender to His Father in unreserved devotion to His will. Such a sacrifice we read is called a "sweet savour" offering. As we daily join our will to His will letting all that is not of Him be burned up or exposed and emptied, our lives are a sweet savour to our God. Even if you should think your life is not having an impact because of limited contact with others, your sweet fragrance rises upward giving testimony both to men and angels.

Notes

[1] Hannah Hurnard, *Hinds' Feet on High Places* (Wheaton, IL: Tyndale), p. 212.

[2] David C. Needham, *Birthright* (Portland, OR: Multnomah), p. 112.

7
Beholding Him Through Circumstances

My husband is a nice, sweet fellow.
His disposition is mild and mellow.
The only time it is not so
Is just the time I need him tho.
If I wake up feeling sad,
He barks at me—he thinks I'm mad.
So when I need him most you see,
He really is no help to me!

Haven't most of us at one time or another felt as my friend Lois' poem so cleverly describes? Most of the women I have known, even wives of prominent sprititual leaders, admit that they have had such thoughts as "If my husband would only . . . then my needs would be met." Such reasoning whether it is concerning something fairly minor or more critical, seems to imply that our God does not know what is happening to us.

Once we turn from our circumstances to beholding Him, we see that "Nothing in all creation is hidden from God's sight" (Heb. 4:13). Therefore, not only does He know our needs, but He has promised that He "will meet all [our] needs according to His glorious riches in Christ Jesus" (Phil. 4:19).

Jesus Reigns
What then must we conclude? Have the circumstances of our lives gotten out of God's control? No—our Lord reigns! He is in control of

everything that happens. David stated this truth emphatically. "Yours, O Lord, is the greatness and the power and the glory and the majesty and the splendor, for everything in heaven and earth is Yours. Yours, O Lord, is the kingdom; You are exalted as head over all" (1 Chron. 29:11).

Our Lord's continual control of all His creation is reiterated by Paul. "All things were created by Him and for Him. He is before all things, and in Him all things hold together" (Col. 1:16-17). God's moment by moment sustaining control keeps our planet operating as He created it to function. He keeps the earth spinning on its axis at 1000 miles per hour. He sustains as the earth with the moon swings around the sun once a year at the rate of 18½ miles per second. It never varies 1/100,000 of a second on this annual trip.[1]

Observing our Lord's sustaining power over His creation caused one of our atheistic American astronauts to concede that there was a supreme Being in control. While standing on the moon looking up at the earth as he'd done many times in reverse, he observed the bodies of water being held to the earth rather than spilling off. He bowed before Christ receiving Him as His Saviour and Lord.

Reigning in Love

Seeing that Jesus is in control and reigning over heaven and earth leads us to accept everything that happens to us as from Him. Receiving everything from Him is easier when we keep in mind how much He loves us (Ps. 86:13). Should a friend throw himself in front of you receiving a bullet intended for you, be killed, and by some miraculous act be brought back to life, would you ever doubt his actions toward you in the future would be anything except for your good? Of course not. He's proven his love by giving his all—his life.

That is what Jesus did for us. He stepped between us and the wrath of God due us. Now our Lord declares, "I know the plans I have for you; plans to prosper you and not to harm you, plans to give you hope and a future" (Jer. 29:11).

What a comfort to know His plans are for our good and nothing can upset them. Job speaks of God's control when he says, "I know that You can do all things; no plan of Yours can be thwarted" (Job 42:2).

God's plans are for our good because we are "as the apple" of His eye (Ps. 17:8). We are so precious to Him that no small detail goes unnoticed or uncared for. "Even the very hairs of your head are all numbered" (Matt. 10:30). That alone is no small job considering that we lose about 100 hairs per day.

The fact of God's goodness and loving care for us is often hard to grasp when things seem to be falling apart all around us. During such times we should recite over and over a verse such as Psalm 100:5: "For the Lord is good and His love endures forever; His faithfulness continues through all generations." Some days I have simply sung over and over the little chorus, "God is good—He is so good to me," till I believed and delighted in the truth. Our old nature programmed our mind to think God doesn't love us. We now have to reprogram our minds with the truth that He does love us.

Remember that anything that comes to us must first come through Him. We have a three-fold protection. Christ lives within us, we are placed in Him, and He is in the Father. Jesus describes this union in these words: "I have given them the glory that You gave Me, that they may be one as We are one. I in them and You in Me" (John 17:22-23). (Compare with Col. 3:1, 3; Gal. 2:20.)

Undivided Heart

Beholding God through our circumstances means by recognizing His control, we receive the "bad" from Him as well as what we see as good. God says, "I form the light and create darkness; I bring prosperity and create disaster; *I, the Lord, do all these things*" (Isa. 45:7).

As David considered his situation he concluded, "I was silent; I would not open my mouth, for *You* are the one who has done this" (Ps. 39:9). Also, when David was cursed by Shimei, who did he receive it from, Shimei or the Lord? He said, "Leave him alone; let him curse, for the Lord has told him to" (2 Sam. 16:11). When Joseph's brothers stood terrified in his presence knowing they had sold him into slavery years earlier, to whom did Joseph credit his being in Egypt? "It was not you who sent me here, but God" (Gen. 45:8). Though the cup that Jesus had to drink had been brought to His lips by Judas through his betrayal, who did He say gave it to Him? "Shall I not drink the cup the Father has given Me?" (John 18:11)

How easy it would have been for Job to have blamed Satan for all his troubles. However, he took the same perspective as David, Joseph, and Jesus when he said, *"The Lord has taken away"* (Job 1:21). These men knew that the secret of peace is in receiving all from God. They mounted higher than their immediate circumstances and saw that God reigns with complete control over all.

Receiving everything from God gives peace as opposed to a man with a divided heart who is looking first to one thing and then another as being responsible for the circumstances in his life. James described such a person as "a double-minded man, unstable in all he does" (James 1:8). We never want to honor or lift up Satan or others by crediting them with the power to control what happens in the lives of God's children. Instead our cry must be "Teach me Your way, O Lord, and I will walk in Your truth; give me *an undivided heart*, that I may fear Your name" (Ps. 86:11).

Enlargement

Why would our reigning Lord allow painful, "bad" things to touch our lives? Our finite minds simply can't grasp all the marvelous ways of our Holy God. However, Psalm 4:1 gives us a clue. "Thou hast *enlarged me* when I was in distress" (KJV). "Bad" things, when used by God, become good because He uses them to enlarge us.

Part of His enlarging process includes pruning us. To do the pruning, God uses people and circumstances as His knife. "Every branch that does bear fruit He trims clean so that it will be even more fruitful (John 15:2). We must look beyond the knife blade and see the loving hand of the Father, who operates with the utmost gentleness and precision. He cautiously uses only the needed hardship to enlarge us so that we can contain and reveal His glory.

God also uses "bad" things to expose the two root sins from which all others spring—pride and unbelief. As they are exposed we can allow Jesus to clean them out by claiming forgiveness based on His work for us at Calvary.

Joseph's life is a good illustration. It wasn't fair that Potiphar's wife betrayed him and had him thrown in prison for a crime he never committed. Yet in God's hands these bad things became good. God used them to empty Joseph of his pride.

Looking back on the story we can see what an arrogant brat Joseph was. He not only wore better clothes than his brothers, and didn't do the hard work they were required to do, but he went around bragging about his dream which showed his brothers bowing before him. The fact that Joseph's brothers or Potiphar's wife had no regard for God didn't frustrate God's plan at all. Instead He used their vindictiveness to accomplish His will in Joseph's life. (See Gen. 37-50.)

God used the Apostle John's difficult circumstances as well as other Christians' persecutions during the 1st century to strengthen their belief in Him. Here was a 90-year-old man exiled on the island of Patmos, hacking rocks out of granite. Did John see the harsh reign of that warped personality Domitian as King? No! He saw Jesus Christ reigning as King. He received it all from His Lord as did the other Christians at that time. God used it to strengthen their belief in Him and prosper His church.

Whether our Father uses people, circumstances, or even Satan to pull weeds of pride and unbelief out of our lives, we know He's the gardener. When His purposes are fulfilled or the weeds are eliminated, He'll set aside the tool He used. In the meantime we have been enlarged to glorify Him as well as receive His blessings.

Embrace with Thanksgiving

One morning Sarah said, "Life seems so fatalistic. I look at my situation and get so discouraged. It seems life is just rolling over me and I'm getting crushed!"

Gradually, as we talked, God showed us that such a view is a negative reaction to His sovereign control. Such a response forgets God's love and the ultimate purpose being fulfilled in our lives while on Planet Earth. Our enemy would have us succumb to such thinking because in doing so we forfeit our sweet fellowship and communion with God. He is robbed of our worship and ministry to Him, and we are robbed of His blessing.

Instead of giving in to the fatalistic idea that life is rolling over us, we must rise up and *embrace life with thanksgiving*. "Thank (God) in everything—no matter what the circumstances may be, be thankful and give thanks; for this is the will of God for you (who are) in Christ Jesus" (1 Thes. 5:18, AMP).

By receiving everything that enters our lives with thanksgiving we are not saying that we are tickled to death that this thing has happened. But we are recognizing our Lord's sovereign control and are completely yielding to Him. We let Him work in us for His good pleasure because He knows what is best.

As we embrace life with a thankful spirit which is lifted up to our God, He develops in us a quiet and gentle spirit. "Your beauty . . . should be that of your inner self, the unfading beauty of *a gentle and quiet* spirit, which is of great worth in God's sight" (1 Peter 3:3-4).

Elaine has embraced this truth faithfully. As a result, God has and is revealing in her a quiet and gentle spirit that not only honors Him but draws others to Himself. When Tom divorced her and remarried, she thanked God. She began thanking Him with an act of her will through hurt and tears till she could behold Him through it all and delight in her thanksgiving. She thanked God for His control and love during Tom's harshness to the children. She thanked God when false stories were spread as past friends and in-laws joined Tom's side.

Faithfully she used the three Rs test to expose the sins that so easily squelch a thankful spirit. She'd ask, "Father, am I (1) resenting You, (2) resisting You, or (3) rebelling against You?" If He showed her that any of these sins were present in her life, she'd confess them, turn back to Him, and melt before Him saying, "Mold me, make me as You see fit. I'm putty in your hands."

How very helpful the three Rs have been as a gauge in my life revealing any willful or defiant spirit. When an unwelcome telephone call, a harsh word, or an unexpected set of circumstances arise, all I have to do is say, "I will not resent, resist, or rebel against You, Lord," and things begin taking their proper perspective.

God has used Elaine's quiet and gentle spirit to draw her children to Himself. Today all three of her children are mature beyond their years embracing God as their God. Elaine's mother-in-law now spends her special days with her and the children. She's seeing how she too can be thankful in spite of her son and new daughter-in-law's rejection. Friends who had forsaken Elaine are gradually gathering in, seeking the peace she exhibits for their own troubled and torn lives.

Beholding God through our circumstances with a thankful spirit is what sustains us through all of life. Greeting the minor happenings of each day with a "Thank you, Jesus" response enables us to embrace more serious, major circumstances with this same spirit.

Jozeca's[2] reaction during imprisonment for her Christianity touched me deeply. When the guard slung their first meal consisting of gray liquid with fish scales floating in it on the floor by the drain which also served as their toilet, the other women winced at the putrid smell and complained. Jozeca said, "We will get down on our knees and thank God for it!" Lifting the cup to her mouth and kissing it she prayed, "Thank you, Lord, for this food which will keep us alive."

Begin each day with a thankful spirit till it becomes a way of life. Start by focusing on the simple, mundane, and often taken for granted areas such as the air we breathe, the ability to serve others, and the privilege of thinking about Him. It is this spirit that raises us to live on a level above our circumstances rather than under them.

Receive as Needed

We can embrace all that comes into our lives with thanksgiving knowing God allows only what we need. That means everyone in our lives is put there by God. One might react with, "But you don't know how different my husband and I are." That's the idea. God never puts two spoons together. He uses two opposites so that as they become "one," their strengths balance out each other's weaknesses.

For instance, I am a talker who not only finds it difficult to conceal my feelings, but who needs to bare my soul before those I am around. On the other hand, DeWitt tires easily of chitchat and has difficulty revealing his innermost self. My talking and urging him to open up only drove us farther and farther apart. Through comments he'd make and observations of his reactions, God showed me to "be still before the Lord and wait patiently for Him" (Ps. 37:7).

When DeWitt's response to my talking at times would seem unnecessarily sharp, God would show me that I needed that exact degree of sternness to break my stubborn will and develop in me a quiet and gentle spirit. It hasn't been easy and my mouth still flops open sometimes when it shouldn't. But it's a joy to see that as I learn to be still and grow in my relationship with the Lord, DeWitt is opening up his inner self more and more. We are now enjoying an intimate closeness far beyond my fondest expectations. We are what each other needs as we receive it from the Lord.

In contrast, my sister Jan finds it much easier to be quiet before the Lord rather than to open up her innermost self. To give her the balance she needs, God is using her husband to force her to work through and verbalize her feelings and convictions. She has to helplessly depend on the Spirit's empowering to open up, just as I do to shut up. Both of us have the husbands we need to turn our weaknesses into strengths, allowing the balanced persons God designed to emerge.

As God was showing me the principle that each of us have exactly what we need in our lives, Sarah came to my mind. I thought, *Since God never gives us one bit more pressure than we need, then our degree of difficulty must be in direct proportion to our stubbornness. But if I tell Sarah this, I'm afraid it might be the straw that'll break the camel's back.*

About that time, Sarah called saying, "While on my knees before the Lord asking *Why*?, He showed me what I was going through was exactly what I needed to break my stubborn, independent spirit."

We rejoiced together. God had shown her the exact truth He was teaching me. It hadn't crushed her, but gave her insight. Progress would be made as she refused to resist, resent, or rebel against God's dealings with her.

This same principle was brought out as Shirley told her story. As a young girl, she defiantly married against her parents' wishes. After wise counsel from a Bible teacher, she began to see that God wanted to use her husband's harsh treatment of her to break her rebellious will. She had refused to submit to God's dealings with her by way of her parents—now He was using her husband. When she submitted to her Lord by way of her husband, God brought about a quiet and gentle spirit that later drew her husband to the right way.

What we think we need is not always what we really need. However, our loving heavenly Father knows what we need and sees that we have it. Lois' new ending to her poem points this out.

> My husband is a nice sweet fellow
> His disposition is mild and mellow
> But when I need him most you see,
> He really is a help to me.

Focus Straight Ahead

Since everything that enters our lives is as a result of divine prescription, our top priority is to keep our eyes fixed on God. We should concentrate on what He is teaching us, rather than trying to help Him straighten out someone else. "Let *your eyes* look right on [with fixed purpose], and let *your gaze* be straight before you. Consider well the path of *your feet,* and let all *your ways* be established and ordered aright. Turn not aside to the right hand or to the left; remove *your foot* from evil" (Prov. 4:25-27, AMP).

Mother and I saw this principle worked out so beautifully through a situation in her life. Each morning and night after my grandmother came home from her volunteer work at the nursing home, she criticized people she knew. The sin of a critical attitude was still fresh in Mother's mind because God had just dealt with her on this and she felt victory had been achieved. She told Grandmother that criticism was sin. But Grandmother only pouted for days then resumed her activity.

As Mother and I prayed about the situation, God began giving insights. We saw that the Holy Spirit was not convicting Grandmother of her sin, so something else must be going on. Then we saw it. Mother was critical of Grandmother's critical spirit. God wasn't through with His lesson to her on criticism. Mother turned her eyes to her path only, confessing her sin of criticism each time it raised its ugly head. She then loved Grandmother as if her speech were ideal.

Shortly after Mother had victory, Grandmother stopped her flood of criticism. Once God had finished using Grandmother in Mother's life, He literally removed her from the situation. My 87-year-old grandmother married the 91-year-old companion she had dreamed of having in her final days. What a joy it was to observe their tender love for each other during a recent visit.

When we realize God is using circumstances to change us, we can stop praying, "God change my circumstances," and pray, "God show me what You want to do in me through this circumstance so I can cooperate."

A quick plea for wisdom went up to God as I recognized Margaret's voice on the phone. "Charles continues to humiliate me. Why does he insist on not doing what he should? He knows better. Won't he ever be yielded to God?"

My response this particular day was as much a shock to me as to her. I said, "No, Margaret, I don't believe he will ever be totally surrendered to God until you are! You see, you think you're God's woman, when in reality you're resisting and resenting everything He brings into your life. Until you can get your eyes off Charles and allow God to use all He brings into your life as His divine prescription to empty you of your self-centeredness, I don't believe God will change your circumstances. He wants to use this to make you completely yielded to Him before He'll bring the same in Charles' life.

My answer was so severe I might not have given it if I'd had time to think about it. However, I knew it was from the Lord because it fit with His Word and was consistent with what He had been teaching me.

Today Margaret is no longer a complainer. Neither has she turned into a "doormat" as some would fear. Instead she is maturing into a beautiful Christian.

All Benefit

Even though we must keep our eyes on our own path, we must not become unhealthily introspective. Sarah shared one day that guilt was haunting her. She was afraid she wasn't learning what God would have her learn, thus prolonging her circumstances. We reviewed John 16:7-11 together till she understood that it was the Holy Spirit's job to point out areas that she needed to turn from. If God wasn't showing her anything as she was regularly in the Word, she should keep on praising and fellowshipping with Him.

God recently gave me a beautiful confirmation of this truth. I had been burdened by DeWitt's lack of compassion for those outside our circle of family and intimate friends. As I prayed about it, God showed me that I was just as imbalanced. My overwhelming passion had been for others. I concluded that since my husband was a Christian and a healthy adult, he didn't need me as much as all those troubled people.

But God showed me that He was using us to balance each other. As I concentrated on becoming as compassionate for DeWitt as I had been for others, He'd take care of DeWitt. God began balancing my life. I enjoyed the intimate companionship DeWitt and I shared so much that I forgot about what God might be doing in his life simultaneously.

Then one day a letter came with a request from a husband to hear DeWitt's side of our marriage. DeWitt wrote the following letter in answer to the request.

Dear Friend,

This is DeWitt. I don't really know how to answer your request. First of all, no one has ever wanted my reply or asked for my help. Secondly, I am not much of a writer or one to give counsel. I would sincerely like to give my version, however.

When we got married, I had no idea what marriage was all about. As time went by it was a sort of good times and bad times. *Well, this must be marriage*, was my conclusion, since my parents were divorced and had always had problems. I later learned a lot of problems would not go away, but there was a way to deal with these.

When our kids became older and the problems of their care were not so great, Darien and I seemed to be having some of our own. As I remember now, these were mostly in communication. As always it seems like the wife maybe doesn't recognize the problem first, but they seem to be the first one to do something about it.

She started feeling a need for more spiritual things and as a result this caused Darien to recognize more the wife she was not. She was getting recognized as a Bible teacher, Sunday School worker, etc. Then later wrote the book, *You Can Be the Wife of a Happy Husband*. Actually, I was a great prospect to practice on because I am very independent and stubborn. But in spite of this, our marriage was really improving, except now I thought she was giving the impression that she was better than me spiritually. This went on probably 2—3 years. Even with these ups and downs, it was still better.

About two years ago, I realized I had been the problem. I had been looking for Darien to do the impossible on me. What a job!

HYMERA COMM. LIBRARY

Now after putting in practice what I had known for so long, which is my personal responsibility as husband and father, coupled with her applying what she teaches, we really have a great marriage. This even carries over into our sons' lives and they are a great testimony to what has happened as a result of all this.

I do not know if this has helped or hindered, but thanks for the opportunity.

Respectfully,
DeWitt

(After DeWitt wrote this letter he shared that just days before the request came, God had convicted him of his lack of compassion for others. When he'd responded to God and made himself available, He immediately gave him an opportunity to reach out. God uses each set of circumstances not only in our lives, but in others' lives that are touched.)

No Room for Failures

God takes our failures and turns them into good for us and for those involved with us. He takes our seemingly wrong choices and weaves them into His overall plan. In other words, we can't fail with God. It is as if He actually uses such things as raw material for erecting His temple within us. For example, God used the ungodly King Saul to develop David into a godly king. When we "fail" with our own children, husband, and others, God's plan is not frustrated. "All things God works for the good of those who love Him, who are called according to His purpose" (Rom. 8:28).

Knowing that God wastes nothing, but is teaching others as He teaches us is a comfort. However, to keep my perspective healthy, I frequently have to ask myself the following questions. *What is my attitude? Am I reflecting an unhealthy, "Oh, what this person puts me through" response? Or is it, "I'm sorry my mate has to go through so much in order for my self-centeredness to be emptied. Lord, let me learn quickly so he won't have to endure so much"?*

What a liberating truth—no failures with God. He wastes nothing! As He is using my husband and others to correct my weaknesses, He is likewise using my shortcomings to develop them.

Acceptance VS Passivity

Receiving everything that comes into our lives with a thankful spirit doesn't mean passivity. Instead it means that once we have thankfully received everything and released any bitterness, resentment, or unforgiveness the Lord reveals, He may direct us to some specific action.

For instance, Judy's husband's domineering nature tended to run roughshod over those he loved, thus having a demoralizing effect by berating their intellect. He didn't realize that his actions weren't expressing his love. This was evidenced one day as they made a business stop. Jack asked Judy to order some stationery while he took care of some other matters. When he returned, he cancelled most of her order and made other choices.

Once the family was back in the car, Judy thought, "He does this all the time. I'll give him five traffic lights before I let him have it!"

As the second and third lights came and went, God got her attention. She allowed Him to drain her of all resentment, bitterness, and unforgiveness. When she was content to do nothing, God prompted her to share with Jack what she'd observed. She knew God had arranged it because not only had the children drifted off to sleep giving them privacy, but her attitude was right. She felt real love for Jack and deep sorrow that she was going to have to share something that would bring hurt to his soul.

Very carefully, she pointed out that often it's more important to say, "I love you" by respecting the decisions one has made upon request than to have one's stationery so precise. Gently she pointed out times he had unintentionally done the same thing with the children. As he thanked her for sharing with him, he said, "I appreciate that very much."

Weeks later when one of their children had been inconsiderate, Judy heard Jack explaining, "Honey, you and I have a problem in this area. Let's see what we can do about it."

How much one can share, when, and how will depend on your husband. As you observe him and look to Jesus for guidance, He will direct.

Elaine understood that receiving everything from God didn't mean that she was not to have legal representation when Tom served her with divorce papers. (See Rom. 13.) She had done all within her power to prevent this action. She'd asked his forgiveness for the areas God had shown her she had failed as his wife. Her changed life had proven her sincerity. Her availability to start rebuilding their marriage was always evident.

Yet when Tom insisted on the divorce, Elaine rested in God's care, never once being vindictive or abusing her privilege of representation by trying to get back at him financially for leaving her. God's gracious care of her continues as Psalm 3:3 expresses. "But You are a shield around me, O Lord, my glorious One, who lifts up my head."

Let's remember—in acceptance lieth peace as we behold Him with thanksgiving! Why? Because "The Lord reigns" (93:1).

Notes

[1] Paul Lee Tan, *Encyclopedia of 7700 Illustrations* (Rockville, MD: Assurance Publishers), p. 350.

[2] Marie Chapian, *Of Whom the World Was Not Worthy* (Minneapolis: Bethany Fellowship), p. 99. Jozeca is one of the main figures in a true story about a family in Europe who withstood war, poverty, and imprisonment for their belief in God.

8
Beholding Him Through Forgiveness

"I hate You, God, for taking the only thing I truly ever loved. How could You? We gave our lives to You. What kind of a God are You anyway? We were active in the church and gave of ourselves to others. We were so happy. I hate You! I hate You! I hate You!"

For 10 minutes or so Larry vented to God, in language unfit for a Sunday School audience, everything that had built up within him during the previous 5 weeks. His lovely wife had died while in his arms as a result of a freak shooting accident. He couldn't cope. This rugged man who could bench press 300-400 pounds, had taken to his bed so weak he could hardly get out. Then one Monday morning he picked up his gun to end it all. Expecting to see the Lord shortly, he decided to simply talk to Him first.

Phases of Reaction

Whether we face a tragedy such as Larry's, rejection and divorce as Elaine has, or something more minor, certain reactions are normal when working through hurt and grief. In the beginning we're usually in a state of shock. We might say, "I just can't believe it has happened. Intellectually I know it did, but I guess I just haven't really accepted it emotionally."

Then our emotional release comes about the time we realize how dreadful our loss is. These emotions *should* be released. Often we may begin to feel depressed and isolated, even having doubts about God. Psychosomatic illnesses may surface. Next, we might panic because we can only think of our loss. Then comes the guilt, followed by hostility and resentment. We may be so overcome with grief that we're unable to return to our usual activities. But gradually hope comes through, and we struggle to readjust to reality.

Everyone who has had a loss or hurt does not necessarily go through each of these stages, nor does he necessarily go through them in this order. However, problems develop when we stay in one phase for an abnormally long time and allow our grief to become morbid. As we recognize that these stages are normal processes which we have to work through, and behold our God during them, we can adjust with the least amount of suffering.

Jesus never condemned Mary and Martha as they grieved over the loss of their brother Lazarus. Instead he joined them. "Jesus wept." Then the Jews said, "See how He loved him!" (John 11:35-36)

Root Problem

Larry recognized that it was God that He couldn't forgive. He didn't like the way God was running his life. For others it isn't always as easy to see that their unforgiveness is really against God rather than other people. However, since Jesus *does* reign, then we must receive all from Him. Not to forgive another person is to not forgive our God. It is saying He had no right to do this in our lives.

Secondary actions (Gal. 6:1-2; Matt. 18:15-17) may need to be taken. The person who has sinned should be led back to the Lord and if necessary make restitution. But we must see that any unforgiveness on our part aims directly at our God.

One day when I was drooping around generally frustrated and feeling resentment mounting toward DeWitt, the Lord brought this thought to my mind. *It is Me you are mad at, not DeWitt! Face it. Deal with it.* Mentally I argued for a few minutes, then I remembered. *My God is in control. He is God, not me, and He can do what He likes! Whatever He does is best for me, and I must yield to Him as God.*

The mounting frustration was a result of not giving Him the right to do as He wanted in my life. My reaction was one of unforgiveness toward God. I had stopped focusing on God and had started looking at my circumstances.

Within a short period of time, DeWitt and I were having sweet fellowship again. But it came only after I became very honest with God and then made the proper adjustment. Other times it has taken longer to know His overflowing joy. Often it seems the longer I turn from Him, the longer it takes to reestablish that soul-satisfying oneness again.

My degree of resistance determines how long I have to read such passages as Job 38—41 and Isaiah 45. "Will the one who contends with the Almighty correct Him? Would you discredit My justice? Would you condemn Me to justify yourself? Do you have an arm like God's and can your voice thunder like His? Then adorn yourself with glory and splendor, and clothe yourself in honor and majesty. Who then is able to stand against Me? Who has a claim against Me that I must pay? Everything under heaven belongs to Me" (Job 40:2, 8-10; 41:10-11). "Woe to him who quarrels with his Maker . . . Does the clay say to the potter, 'What are you making?' . . . Do you question Me about My children, or give orders about the work of My hands?" (Isa. 45:9, 11)

Such passages serve as an equalizer to me. Once again I begin to see that God is the Creator deserving the worship and obedience from His creature. With Job I then say, "Surely I spoke of things I did not understand, things too wonderful for me to know. Therefore I despise myself and repent in dust and ashes" (Job 42:3, 6).

Pride Blocks Forgiveness

Why would anyone not embrace all that happens with a spirit of forgiveness? Pride, the sin that tops God's list of most hated sins (Prov. 6:16-19), is often the reason. To forgive another means we must also recognize our own fallibility. That is difficult for a proud person.

Jesus spoke clearly about such a person in the parable of the servant who owed the king the equivalent of $10 million. He could not pay, and pleaded for mercy. The king forgave him all his debt. But as soon as the servant was released, he went to a man who owed him the equivalent of $2,000, grabbed him by the throat, and demanded instant payment. The man didn't have the money and fell to his knees begging for time. The king's servant refused and had the man thrown in jail till the debt could be paid in full.

When the king heard, he called the servant and said, "You wicked servant, I cancelled all that debt of yours because you begged me to. Shouldn't you have had mercy on your fellow servant just as I had on you?" Then the angry king sent the man to the torture chamber till he had paid every last penny owed. Jesus warned, "This is how My heavenly Father will treat each of you unless you forgive your brother from your heart." (See Matt. 18:21-35.)

Forgiving a husband who rejected you for another woman as Elaine's husband did, may be harder in many ways than losing your mate through death. However, Elaine knew she had to genuinely forgive Tom and his new wife from her heart, or she could not expect God's forgiveness. "For if you forgive men when they sin against you, your heavenly Father will also forgive you. But if you do not forgive men their sins, your Father will not forgive your sins" (6:14-15).

Pride often expresses itself as, "But I haven't committed adultery or done anything as bad to them as they have to me. I don't deserve such treatment." Oswald Chambers' response to this attitude is right to the point. He says, "If I have never been a backguard, the reason is a mixture of cowardice and the protection of civilized life; but when I am undressed before God, I find my sins are just as despicable as the other person's." [1]

Often the bitterness and resentment that result in unforgiveness have mounted up so slowly that we aren't aware of how hostile we are or what we haven't forgiven. An unkind word, a disappointment, or a hurt may be the beginning of trouble. Therefore we are cautioned, "Exercise foresight and be on the watch . . . in order that no root of resentment [rancor, bitterness, or hatred] shoot forth and cause trouble and bitter torment" (Heb. 12:15, AMP).

The following symptoms often indicate an unforgiving spirit.

1. God seems so distant.
2. The fruit of the Spirit is not evident in my life.
3. I have no desire to pray.
4. I have no desire to read God's Word.
5. There is no joy in my life.
6. I don't enjoy fellowship with others.
7. I feel that others are against me.

8. I'm bored with everything.
9. I'm haunted by someone I'd like to forget.
10. I can't think of anything pleasant about certain individuals.
11. My life is characterized by complaints.
12. I feel drained emotionally.
13. I resent, resist, and rebel against certain people and situations in my life.
14. I often feel, "I don't deserve this!"
15. I want to see someone else suffer because they've caused me pain.

Should any of these symptoms describe your life, turn to God with the following prayer. "Search me, O God, and know my heart; test me and know my anxious thoughts. See if there is any offensive way in me, and lead me in the way everlasting" (Ps. 139:23-24).

As God brings people and circumstances to your mind, carefully deal with each one. Review the hurt and recognize that God permitted that incident because He wants to bring about good to you as a result of it. This situation might have been the only way He could expose your bitterness, resentment, or unforgiving spirit. He loves you so much He wants to empty it all out of you.

Remember that Jesus paid for the other person's sin as well as your sin while He hung on the cross. Then forgive your offender and accept God's forgiveness for yourself. Next, thank Him for the event and continue thanking Him till you are delighting in His forgiveness.

No Conditions for Forgiveness

We might think, "I would forgive that person if only he or she would ask me to forgive," or "How can I forgive someone who doesn't want to be forgiven?" Jesus did. As He hung on the cross, He said, "Father, forgive them, for they do not know what they are doing" (Luke 23:34).

One day Sarah said, "How long am I to continue forgiving my husband?" Our human reasoning might conclude with Peter that 7 times was a gracious plenty. But our Lord answered, "I do not say to you, up to seven times, but up to seventy times seven" (Matt. 18:22, NASB). Should we add up and say, "OK—after 490 times we don't have to forgive anymore," we've missed the message.

Sarah was beginning to see that real forgiveness accepts a person just as he is, even if he continues to do the thing that hurts us. Our conditions for forgiveness (he must see his error, admit his guilt, ask our forgiveness, and promise to change) simply are not Christ's!

"But," Sarah continued, "isn't my forgiveness condoning his actions?" That question could be answered with another question. Was Jesus approving of His murderers' actions? Of course not! Besides Sarah's husband, Steve, was well aware that she didn't approve of his actions. By forgiving Steve, she was able to respond to him as her Lord had responded to her. She gave him a firsthand exposure to God's nature in action.

Sarah had one last question. "My continual forgiveness seems almost like letting him get by with his sin. Shouldn't I punish him in some way?" God's Word says, "Do not take revenge, my friends, but leave room for God's wrath, for it is written: 'It is mine to avenge; I will repay,' says the Lord. Do not be overcome by evil, but overcome evil with good" (Rom. 12:19, 21).

If Sarah had responded with unforgiveness, she would have been trying to overcome evil with evil. Instead, "Those who suffer according to God's will should *commit themselves to their faithful Creator and continue to do good*" (1 Peter 4:19).

Not only does responding to evil with good fulfill God's command to us, but we will know the joy that being in His will brings. Brian, our middle son, recently experienced the joy and reward of repaying evil with good. His eyes sparkled as he related the incident. "During our soccer game today when an opponent and I collided, he let me have it in abusive language. Rather than lash back at him as usual, I turned to him in love without any frustration and said, 'I was simply playing my position to the best of my ability without any intention of hurting you.' Then I proceeded to play the game without any anger that has so often been present under similar circumstances. After the game he came up and apologized to me." Brian experienced the difference it makes inside and out to repay evil with good.

Unforgiveness—Putrid Aroma

Unforgiveness releases a poisonous, putrid aroma in us and through us. The horrible stench released by unforgiveness became vividly apparent to me one day as our oldest son, Craig, and I were being checked out at a local grocery store. To the astonishment of all around, a middle-aged woman, repulsive in physical appearance, started verbally attacking a man her own age as he entered the store. She pranced back and forth calling him a liar, a cheat, and a low-down snake. Then she threatened to kill him. She taunted him by saying, "Come on and hit me if you dare!"

When we left the store, I felt very dirty as a result of simply being exposed to such poison. Upon getting into the car, I wanted to simply weep and weep and weep. I realized if the poison just released by unforgiveness had affected me so tremendously, think how much more horrendous our sin is to our holy God! No wonder Jesus, who had never known the stench of sin cried out, "My God, My God, why have You forsaken Me?" (Ps. 22:1)

Then I remembered that our bodies are the temples of a holy God who lives within us (1 Cor. 6:19). Anytime we refuse to confess our unforgiveness, we are subjecting Him afresh to the poisonous stench of sin. In effect we are doing the same thing the Jews did who were warned about their deliberate sinning. We are trampling the Son of God underfoot and being an insult to His very work on the cross. "How much more severely do you think a man deserves to be punished who has trampled the Son of God underfoot, who has treated as an unholy thing the blood of the covenant that sanctified him, and who has insulted the Spirit of grace?" (Heb. 10:29)

Immediately, I begged the Lord to keep me sensitive to any unforgiveness in my life so that I could drop it like a hot coal. Never do I want to trample Jesus' work on my behalf by not applying it to sin He exposes in me.

Any unforgiveness that we coddle may not be as obviously putrid to us as the woman's display in the grocery store. Since we dress nicer and say words that are socially acceptable, we don't always recognize our unforgiveness as sin. But our unforgiveness is just as repugnant in our Lord's eyes as that woman's was.

When our sons were smaller, we refused to allow them to contaminate those around them with their poisonous bad attitudes. If they didn't shape up after being corrected, they were sent to their rooms with this explanation. "Son, go to your room till your attitude is right.

You have no right to contaminate the rest of the family by spewing out your poisonous attitude on us.'' Whether we're young or old we must learn that sin pollutes.

Our forgiveness not only contaminates others but it causes defilement within. Doctors estimate that 85 percent of the patients in hospitals are there because of the damage done to their physical bodies through resentment, bitterness, and unforgiveness. God designed our bodies to function as we are Spirit controlled. When we insist on being controlled by the power of sin in the flesh, our body chemistry and glandular functions are thrown into havoc. A doctor can sometimes cut out the physical decay caused by unforgiveness, but the destruction will not be arrested till we've made peace with God. Departing from evil and revering the Lord brings good health (Prov. 3:7-8).

Forgiveness Releases Power in Us

One summer morning about 3 A.M. I found myself wide awake. (By the way, should you find yourself awake in the early hours assume that God wants your attention unless there is another obvious reason. You might even need to slip out of bed and let Him speak to you through His Word.) As I turned to God He brought to my mind an unkindness I had done years earlier to DeWitt's dad. I had not forgiven him for wrongs he had committed against his family. As a result our relationship with him was severed. Immediately, I confessed my sin to God. But He showed me I must also ask Mr. Cooper's forgiveness and seek to restore that relationship.

Several days later when I approached DeWitt with my decision, he said that he had also been feeling that we should do the same thing. God is so faithful. He had likewise prepared my father-in-law's heart, enabling him to graciously forgive us and restore our fellowship with him.

Sin blocks our relationship with God and any resulting joy and peace He wants to give us (Ps. 66:18). As we forgive and are forgiven, God's power is released in and through us—allowing us to know His peace, joy, and contentment. I am convinced that I would not have experienced the joy I described in chapter 1 if I had not forgiven and sought forgiveness a few months before.

Forgiveness Releases Power Through Us

Our forgiveness not only releases God's power *in* us, but *through* us. We release His power of forgiveness by showing that we have no resentment toward the person who has hurt us. Jesus demonstrated His lack of resentment for Judas by giving him the first sop during the last supper. The one to whom the host gave the first sop was paid honor in Jesus' day. Jesus was not only pointing out that Judas would betray Him, but He was showing Judas that He loved him and held no resentment against him.

Being the vessel through which God's forgiveness flows is not always easy, as Elaine can verify. Soon after her divorce she wrestled with the decision of whether to approve her children's visit to their father's new home. Would the new wife mistreat them? Would their going mean her approval of the situation? Should she seek to get back at Tom for his rejection of her by making it harder for him to see their children? Shouldn't she keep them away from him for fear his newly-embraced morals might affect them? On and on the doubts, mixed emotions, and temptations tugged at her.

Finally, Elaine realized that evil can only be overcome by good. This didn't mean that proper morals were not taught to her children. She knew God was holding her responsible for teaching them the best she could and, most of all, setting an example before them. Part of her example was to exhibit before them forgiveness void of any resentment or bitterness and trust God for the results. She reminded her children that they too must continue to love their dad without any resentment, even though he had hurt them all deeply.

Jesus has worked in a variety of ways to solve the problems for the best of all concerned. Elaine's children still see their dad periodically, but not at his home as much because his new wife tired of the inconvenience. The children are kind and thoughtful to him, but certainly not drawn to his ways. They all continue to pray for the day that he will return to the Lord as they remain available to love him as much as he will allow.

Our lack of forgiveness can be a hindrance to God's working in a particular situation. Now, we must not get a distorted view of our importance. God can always bypass us if our hearts have become hardened, and accomplish His purposes in other ways. But often He uses a circumstance to expose our unforgiveness and waits for us to deal with our sin before He changes the situation.

Louise had faithfully requested prayer at every prayer meeting for over a year that Rick, her unsaved husband, would become a Christian. Nothing happened . . . till she faced her unforgiveness and forgave. Not only had she resented his not going to church, but she had harbored bitterness, resentment, and unforgiveness against him for many things.

Within days after Louise confessed her unforgiveness and reached out to Rick in genuine love, he came to know Christ personally. Her unforgiveness seemed to be hindering God's working in Rick's life. We should note, however, that Louise's repentance was genuine and not a manipulative tactic to get God to change a circumstance. Remember that God knows our hearts. We don't dare play games with Him.

Unforgiveness Blocks Full Flow of Mercy

Our sin of unforgiveness blocks God's full flow of mercy to others. God's plan is to display His nature through us, but sin limits that display. In Louise and Rick's case, Rick did not have the full exposure to God's love to him since one of God's primary tools, his wife, was blocked because of sin. (See 1 Peter 3:1-2.)

The fact that our sin can affect others is pointed out in God's Word. "Make every effort to live in peace with all men and to be holy; *without holiness no one will see the Lord.* See to it that *no one misses the grace of God and that no bitter root grows up to cause trouble and defile many*" (Heb. 12:14-15).

Mary Lou and John separated for the purpose of ending their marriage. Mary Lou went to her parents' home in another state to rest. On the way, she stopped to purchase a book on how to deal with divorce. My first book, *You Can Be the Wife of a Happy Husband*, caught her eye. She didn't want to read it, but prompting from within insisted.

As she read, the Holy Spirit convicted her of many personal sins as well as how she had failed as John's wife. Many miles away from John, she confessed her sins, forgave him for the many ways he had hurt her, and resolved to make amends if at all possible. Weeks later when she saw John, she realized he was also a changed man. As they compared their stories, Mary Lou was awed that John's change began almost immediately after her forgiveness and change of attitude toward him had taken place.

Then there was Sue. Her husband was a military man and seldom home. She was well thought of as a business woman and a Christian worker in their home town. She had managed to keep Ted's heavy drinking and carousing concealed from friends, neighbors, and family even when he was home on furlough. Then retirement time approached. Would he return home to humiliate the family and tear down all she'd built up in the past 25 years? She'd prayed for years that Ted would change his ways, yet nothing had happened.

She was desperate. On her face before her Lord, she pleaded as she had pleaded in the past. Finally, in the wee hours of that Wednesday morning she gave up and relinquished the whole situation into Jesus' hands. She forgave her husband of all his hurtful ways and was willing to face anything with thanksgiving that Jesus allowed to enter her life. She would stand by her man and love him, forgive him, and be what he needed—regardless of the price tag.

Two months later she received a letter from her husband explaining a tremendous change that had happened in his life. He had waited this long to tell her because he wanted to be sure it would last. He recounted to her that one Wednesday morning in the early hours he felt as if he'd been released from a great bondage and with the release he'd never wanted another drink or had the desire to carouse as before. As she checked her calendar, it was the same Wednesday she had forgiven him and entrusted him to God's care.

"How" of Forgiveness

What a priceless privilege not to be in bondage to the cruel shackles of unforgiveness. Because of Christ's work on the cross Booker T. Washington's words can be true for us. "No man is able to force me so low as to make me hate him." Mrs. M. L. Carpenter gives a beautiful illustration in *The Land of His Love*,[2] of one's ability through Christ to forgive.

"The wife of a Zulu chief attended a Salvation Army meeting and heard and responded to the call of Jesus. When her husband heard of this he forbade her to go again on pain of death. However, eager to hear more about Jesus, she dared to go, and when her husband knew of this he met her on her return journey and beat her so savagely that he left her for dead. By and by his curiosity moved him to go back and look for her. She was not where he had left her, but he noticed broken twigs and found her lying under a bush. Covering her with his cruel eyes he leered, "And what can your Jesus Christ do for you now?" She opened her eyes, and looking at him, said gently, "He helps me to forgive you!"

No one can rob us of the joy of forgiveness except ourselves. "But how do I forgive?" you may ask. The *how* of forgiveness is through our will, the rudder of our life. We are responsible for the set of this rudder; once we have willed a course of action, God will be responsible for our feelings as we trust those to Him.

Begin by (1) venting any pent-up emotions to Jesus. Honestly lay it all before Him. Take as long as necessary. (2) Ask Jesus to show you the ugliness of your unforgiveness and to give you a repentant spirit. Then confess your sin (1 John 1:9), and receive His forgiveness. (3) Turn back to Him, trusting Him to be your very life (Col. 2:6; Gal. 2:20). (4) Reach out to the person who has offended you, responding to them with kindness and compassion as if nothing had happened. (5) Thank Him for the event and continue thanking Him until you are delighting in His forgiveness. With these actions you are fulfilling Christ's command in Ephesians 4:30-32. "Do not grieve the Holy Spirit. . . . Get rid of all bitterness, rage and anger, brawling and slander, along with every form of malice. Be kind and compassionate to one another, *forgiving each other, just as in Christ God forgave you.*"

Forgiveness should be easier when we remember that it is God we are ultimately forgiving. He loves us more than we love ourselves and He never ever allows anything to touch our lives that is not for our good. If we are going to behold Him and know His joy, we have no choice but to forgive.

How to Forget

You might say, "I want to forgive and forget but I can't seem to erase my offender's sin from my mind. All I can do is think about it day after day. What did I do to cause this? Why did this happen to me?''

When you realize that such attitudes and statements generally arise from either self-pity or an underlying desire to make the offender suffer for his sins, you know you must turn them loose. Confess your self-pity as sin and receive what has happened from God, allowing Him to expose and empty you of your self-centeredness and draw you closer to Him. Remember that Christ suffered for your offender's sins and yours and neither man nor God may require further atonement.

The genuineness of your forgiveness will be evidenced in the fruit of your actions. Matthew 3:8 states, "Produce fruit in keeping with repentance.'' Part of your fruit should be the willingness to forget. Of course, the granting of forgiveness does not instantly produce forgetfulness. But if you are not forgetting, it is because you are actively remembering.

How do you forget an offense committed against you? Begin by never reminding the offender of his offense again. That means no more, "See you haven't really changed. You did this same thing four years ago!'' Or, "I remember when you. . . .'' Don't dig up past mistakes and gnaw on them. Next, don't tell others of the offense. Resist the temptation to repeat it even under the guise of giving a prayer request. Lastly, do not dwell on the offense again. Should the thought walk across your mind, which it probably will, immediately apply the three steps set forth in Philippians 4:6-9.

First place the problem in God's hands and thank Him that He's taking care of it. Then focus your mind on whatever is true, noble, right, pure, lovely, admirable, excellent, or praiseworthy. As you faithfully apply these two steps, you can expect "the peace of God, which transcends all understanding, will guard your hearts and your minds in Christ Jesus'' (v. 7). Finally, verse 9 reminds us that this must be practiced. How often? As often as necessary! As past unpleasantness is handled in this way, the thought will occur less and less till it is forgotten.

Forgiveness Deepens Love

True forgiveness does not erect any walls to prevent future hurts. Instead you love as if nothing had happened. This is really a deeper love, because the hurt *did* happen—but forgiveness wrapped in love covered it. The vulnerability that you are willing to have, God will use to help you "to grasp how wide and long and high and deep is the love of Christ, and to know this love that surpasses knowledge—that you may be filled to the measure of all the fullness of God" (Eph. 3:18-19). Perhaps nothing else, except your hurt, could have expanded you to experience or know His love to such a degree. What a small price to pay for such a fabulous blessing!

Your offender, then, becomes your friend enabling you to dwell deeply in God and be enlarged to grasp and contain His love. Your offender has allowed you to be emptied of any self-centeredness through the hurtful situation and filled more with the fullness of God. By forgiving, remaining vulnerable, and continuing to reach out in love, you experience love to a depth not possible otherwise.

We will know God's forgiveness has been completed in us when we can genuinely greet our offender in heaven with a warm embrace and a spontaneous "I'm so glad you are here!" Better still, should your paths cross while on earth, honestly encompass him with your love through equally appropriate words or actions. Our Lord promises that "the fruit of righteousness will be peace; the effect of righteousness will be quietness and confidence forever" (Isa. 32:17).

Notes

[1] Oswald Chambers, *My Utmost for His Highest* (Toronto: McClelland & Stewart Limited), p. 208.

[2] Walter B. Knight, *Knights' Master Book of New Illustrations* (Grand Rapids: Eerdmans), p. 228.

9
Beholding Him Through Open Ears and Eyes

"What are you discussing together as you walk along?" Jesus asked two of His followers as they walked on their way to a village called Emmaus.

"Are you the only one living in Jerusalem who doesn't know the things that have happened there in these days?" One of them, named Cleopas asked Him.

"What things?" He asked.

"About Jesus of Nazareth," they replied. They proceeded to tell Him of Jesus' crucifixion and the discovery of His empty tomb that morning. Jesus explained to them that this was all fulfillment of Scripture. After accepting their invitation to stay the night with them, He broke bread with them and *"their eyes were opened and they recognized Him*, and He disappeared from their sight."

Immediately they returned to Jerusalem and told the Eleven. While they were doing so, Jesus suddenly stood among them.

As Jesus talked with them concerning Himself and the last three days' events, He said, "This is what I told you while I was still with you: Everything must be fulfilled that is written about Me in the Law of Moses, the Prophets, and the Psalms." Then He opened their minds so they could understand the Scriptures. (See Luke 24:13-45.)

His Handiwork—Priceless Rare Exhibits
The disciples of Jesus saw, but didn't recognize Him. They heard Him, but didn't know His voice. Then Jesus opened their ears to hear

and unveiled their eyes to see the truth about Himself.

The marvels of the optic wonder of the eye which our Lord created are astounding. The eye can see light from the stars of which the nearest is 25 billion miles away! In the dark the eye's sensitivity increases 100,000 times; one can detect a faint glow, less than a thousandth as bright as a candle's flame.[1]

Our amazement continues upon consideration of the acoustic wonder of the human ear—a receiver capable of handling over 73,000 vibrations per second and is only 1/4 inch long and 1/250 inch in thickness. The inner ear is like a keyboard with 15,000 keys, because that is the number of different tones that can be detected.[2]

As astounding as God's creations of the eye and ear are, they don't compare to the wonder accomplished when He gives us insight into Himself and His ways. Just as Jesus opened His disciples' eyes on the day of His resurrection, He is opening eyes today giving understanding that we may know Him.

Jesus draws each of us to Himself (John 6:44). He reveals to us who He is, just as He did to Simon Peter when Jesus asked him who He was. Peter said, " 'You are the Christ, the Son of the living God.' Jesus replied, 'Blessed are you, Simon son of Jonah, for this was not revealed to you by man, but by My Father in heaven'" (Matt. 16:16-17). All the daily insights and understanding that we receive come from our Lord. "A man can receive only what is given him from heaven" (John 3:27). Therefore each of us is a product of His marvelous divine labor.

With this in view, others take on a precious new dimension. No longer can another be viewed with contempt, indifference, or lack of marvel. Instead we see each other as products of our Lord's craftsmanship. He is in the process of opening our eyes and ears giving enlightenment to our hearts as He conforms us to His image. "For we are God's [own] handiwork [His workmanship]" (Eph. 2:10, AMP). (See Rom. 8:29.)

Others, then, become to us an unveiling of God's magnificent art work. Therefore, we should treat them with an awesome, tender reverence knowing that God is at work. Carefully we observe His strokes in another's life so as to learn more about Him. We discover with excitement how Jesus has worked in their lives, and what He has taught them—knowing that He has given them insights into wonders we haven't yet seen. With tender love we make ourselves available to be of use to the Master in His fashioning of another, should He so choose to honor us.

Not only should believers be treated with an awesome tenderness, but non-believers also. God may be using His loving nature flowing through us to reveal Himself to them. All people then become priceless exhibits in God's art gallery. Some are at a stage to manifest more of His likeness than others. Some are still in the process of being drawn to Him. But all display His glory and teach us more about Him.

The Spirit—The Life Changer

How liberating to know that others as well as ourselves are a result of His workmanship brought about by His Spirit. It is His Spirit, therefore, that is the issue not us. It is His Spirit that opens eyes and ears convicting of sin, righteousness, and judgment—not us (John 16:8).

The Holy Spirit shows us that our main sin is unbelief in Jesus Christ's sufficiency. He gives understanding that being in Christ is the only basis for our right standing with God. He illuminates our hearts to the truth that Satan's power is broken and he has no more authority over us. (See John 16:9-11.)

This emancipating truth that the Spirit alone can accomplish life-changing results began to open up for me as Janet and I ate lunch. As she told me how she had come to know Christ personally, Janet said, "One day after attending a Bible study I asked the teacher once again to pray for my mother. She came back with, 'Janet, have you ever considered trusting the Lord for your mother?'"

Janet said that those words pounded upon her heart with such conviction that when she got home she fell to her knees by her bed. As she prayed, she saw that she had never personally trusted the Lord for herself. She did that day.

The Bible teacher could take no credit for an orderly, flawless Gospel presentation. Now we should always be well prepared and conscientiously clear in giving the plan of salvation. But even that doesn't produce life-changing results. Only God's Spirit does! He can use a precise explanation or He can use something that wasn't even meant for that purpose at all, as He did with Janet.

Doesn't that give freedom? The pressure is off for those of us who get sweaty palms and a rash from anxious worry that we will say or do the wrong thing. We simply prepare ourselves as best we can. Then, as the Lord leads while we are beholding Him in our daily fellowship, He does the life changing. Sometimes He gives us the joy of knowing that He is using us. At other times He uses us in ways in which we are totally unaware. But whatever the case, He does it all!

One day I was heavily burdened because I could not understand DeWitt's reactions in a particular situation. As I drove to the grocery store, I pondered our situation. Before long I was absorbed in the drama theater on the car radio. By the time I'd reached the grocery store, the secular program was drawing to a close and so was my frustration. While listening to that program, the Lord had opened my understanding so that I could see DeWitt's feelings in the situation. I sat in the car weeping and rejoicing. Weeping because I understood how hurtful my actions had been and how they had affected DeWitt— and rejoicing that Jesus had opened my eyes. The secular radio program could take no credit. The glory had to be our Lord's.

By now, confirmation was experientially mounting that the Spirit was the issue, not me. He can take something that is inanimate, animate, secular, or religious to teach His truths to a hungry heart. He is the one who draws people to Himself, makes them hungry, and fills their appetites. What a God! Praise His holy name!

How should this truth affect our relationship with the people God places in our lives? We should be liberated from scheming, arguing, coercing, or entrapping in order to bring about spiritual growth in others. We simply display God's life to them, treating them the way God treats us, and let Him draw, woo, and perfect them to His image.

This means that an unsaved husband won't see a Scripture verse written across the bathroom mirror or a pamphlet tumbling out of his lunch bag or lying on his pillow when he goes to bed. Our job as wives is not to habitually quote Scriptures, insert neat truths that speak to our husbands' obvious weaknesses, or point out that our mates aren't reading their Bibles or praying often enough. God didn't give us to our mates to be a live-in Billy Graham, but as their companions.

At precisely the right time God will draw that loved one to Himself. He may see a leaflet in a public restroom, read it, and receive Christ as

Saviour. He may meet a Christian on an airplane who will share with him. Or the Lord may convict him of his condition while camping out all by himself. But we can be sure, God's timing will be exactly right and the understanding He gives will be life-changing.

One day as I was driving around the perimeter highway that circles Atlanta, I approached the LaVista Road exit. The radio station I was listening to faded out and another came through. The competitor's radio tower at the location began interfering with the reception of my program.

Then I saw a neat comparison. When I try to do the Holy Spirit's work in others' lives, I cause interference just like that radio station was doing. My manipulation and carefully planned injections of spiritual truths cause static and make it harder for the Holy Spirit to get through to the person.

Sometimes we get an exaggerated view of our own importance. We think that the world will fall apart without us. Such a pressure was heavy on my shoulders when I stopped teaching in 1976. I saw marriages falling apart at a disturbing rate and was overwhelmed with guilt because I knew I could share solutions.

Then one day the Lord opened my eyes. I saw I was not indispensable. He could use me or not use me—but either way His plan would move right along. He had given me a message and it had been made transferable. Those that were teachable would respond and He would open their eyes and ears. I was to concentrate on learning to dwell deeply in Him and carry out my priorities with my husband and family. How liberating to see Him as the all-sufficient God that He is!

An Effective Witness

Since an unsaved person does not understand spiritual truths (1 Cor. 2:14), a *life* that talks often makes more of an impression on a mate, than a *mouth* that talks. Peter reminds us of this basic truth. "They may be won over *without talk by the behavior* of their wives" (1 Peter 3:1).

What kind of behavior should a wife exhibit toward her mate? "She will comfort, encourage, and do him only good as long as there is life within her" (Prov. 31:12, AMP). We learn that comforting means being understanding when he has to work 16 hours a day. We do all we can to make his short stay at home the best part of his day. We encourage him by expressing our appreciation for his hard work rather than reminding him that we had to set his picture on the table at dinner time so the children could remember what their daddy looked like. We point out his good qualities and accept him just as he is. We show him that he's the most important person in all our earthly relationships.

He will begin enjoying being around a person who no longer criticizes him, doesn't complain, and generally displays contentment where discontentment used to reign. He will see a companion who is committed to fulfilling her God given role as long as there is life within her, whether or not she sees visible results. Not only will your mate be drawn to you, his wife, but he will want to know what has made the difference in your life.

God used Tricia's quietly lived out testimony to set off a chain of events that drew others to Himself. After reading my book, *You Can Be the Wife of a Happy Husband*, she set about to apply the principles in her marriage. Not only was there a great transformation in her and Wade's relationship, but her mother was fascinated with what she was observing. After several months, she asked Tricia to explain the change she'd noticed. Tricia's mother was given the book and likewise quietly started being the companion to her husband that God had designed her to be.

Several months passed when one night Tricia's mom and dad were sitting in the den talking. Dad laid his head in Mom's lap. As she caressed his head, he started asking her to explain the peace and contentment he'd seen in her life lately. Mom didn't jump up and start preaching with an air of "I've waited so long for this time—now I'll unload all I know!" But she gently and carefully shared that knowing Christ as her personal Saviour and allowing Him to live in and through her had brought about the change. She kept to the point sharing only pertinent information. Dad said, "I want that too!" Together they knelt by the sofa and Dad became a child of God.

Tricia's mom didn't say to her husband, "Dad, you sure have been top sinner on the Wednesday prayer list for months now. Glad you finally came around!" She simply rejoiced with him, sharing his excitement with a heart silently lifted up to God for His magnificent job of opening ears and eyes.

In a similar situation you might be tempted to say, "Oh, I knew that would happen all along. God told me it would." Such statements can give you an air of self-righteousness. Now, I'm not referring to Spirit-controlled sharing at the proper time of a confirmation God has given you concerning another. But it could have been Joseph's inappropriate sharing of his dream concerning his brothers' future bowing down to him, coupled with an air of "I'm special" that flamed their resentment. (See Gen. 37.) Such attitudes melt away when we remember that only Jesus opens eyes and ears—ours and others'. To the ones that Jesus gives added insight much more is required.

When sharing spiritual insights, care should be exercised not to come across with an "I've already learned that" or "You don't have it quite right" attitude. Remember, only Jesus opens ears and eyes. Rejoice over common understanding without trying to force another issue.

Often a wife expects a spiritual oneness with her mate that in reality can be experienced only in her relationship with Jesus. So when Jesus gives a fantastic insight, relish in the understanding with Him. Savor it—bask in it! Should He want you to share it, He will give the opportunity. But don't be disappointed if equal enthusiasm isn't shared. God has to give such illumination.

If your mate is trusting and praising the Lord as a way of life, you will have more liberty to openly share with and before him. If he is not intimately walking with the Lord, he may be turned off by your spiritual verbalizations. Sometimes a man that is insecure in his relationship with his wife is threatened by her talk about her relationship with Jesus. As ridiculous as it may seem, the Lord can become his competitor. In such cases the wife must concentrate on pointing out her husband's good qualities—accepting him like he is and proving to him that he is number one above all earthly relationships. Her verbalizations should center on her husband while she carries on her fellowship with Jesus within her inner sanctuary.

A wife's habitual talk about her relationship with Christ can also be very convicting to her mate if he does not have that intimate a relationship with Christ. Of course, she shouldn't hide her relationship with Christ, but she shouldn't flaunt it either. Our mates are to be ministered to. They want our attention, respect, and admiration—not because Jesus tells us to give them those things—but because we *want* to. In that way they are drawn to Christ, not driven away as constant nagging tends to do. Our job is to comfort and encourage, not convict. That's the Holy Spirit's job. As we minister to our husbands as companions according to their interests, then Christ will do the rest.

Ask God to help you stay sensitive to your mate's needs and to relate to him effectively. "If any of you lacks wisdom, he should ask God, who gives generously to all without finding fault, and it will be given to him" (James 1:5).

Joy of Belief

Whether you can share freely, infrequently, or very little with your mate concerning spiritual matters is not the basis of your overflowing joy. Such joy comes through beholding God though the situation, knowing He alone opens eyes and ears and that He will accomplish His priceless masterpiece in a way that will glorify Himself.

The centurion had such faith in our Lord. We hear him saying to Jesus, " 'Lord, my servant lies at home paralyzed and in terrible suffering.'

"Jesus said to him, 'I will go and heal him.'

"The centurion replied, 'Lord, I do not deserve to have You come under my roof. But just say the word, and my servant will be healed.'

"Then Jesus said to the centurion, 'Go! It will be done just as you believed it would' " (Matt. 8:6-8, 13).

As we behold God by looking straight through our problems to His power and sufficiency, He is released to work in the situation for which we are trusting Him. Unbelief limits Him (13:58). But as we trust in Him, we can have confidence that "nothing is impossible with God" (Luke 1:37).

To Others as to Jesus

Do you sometimes have trouble loving and respecting others with whom you have regular contact? Remember that the way you respond to others is really the way you're responding to Jesus. Jesus said, "Truly, I tell you, in as far as you did it to one of the least of these My brethren, you did it to Me" (Matt. 25:40, AMP).

I can see that clearly when I remember that other Christians are God's temple. (See 1 Cor. 3:16-17.) If a person is not a Christian, Christ desires to draw that person to Himself. Our actions can enhance His work as we display His nature through us.

In view of this we should look through another's area of weakness and literally respond to them as we would to our Lord. As we do so, others take on a preciousness and value perhaps not before realized. Not loving others in such a way is evidence that we really don't love God. "If anyone says, 'I love God,' yet hates his brother, he is a liar. For anyone who does not love his brother, whom he has seen, cannot love God, whom he has not seen. And He has given us this command: Whoever loves God must also love his brother (1 John 4:20-21).

Earthly Bride VS Heavenly Bride

The married woman should view her husband as a priceless, precious treasure through which she values God's working. God has placed her husband in a place of leadership over her to protect, bless, and give her direction. (See 1 Cor. 11:3; Eph. 5:22-24.) Therefore, the way she responds to her mate is indirectly the way she is responding to her Lord. As the wife is willing to let God use her husband in her life to empty her of self-centeredness, pride, and unbelief, she will not only begin to enjoy a sweet oneness with her mate, but will be developing the necessary qualities for being part of Jesus' bride (the church) for eternity.

With respect and reverence we should attentively listen to our Lord through our mates. That doesn't mean that literally everything your man says is accurate, but it does mean God is using him in your life for your good. For instance, if he calls you a lazy good-for-nothing idiot that doesn't mean that you are one. Turn to God and ask Him if any of the accusations are legitimate.

Have you neglected your responsibilities unnecessarily? Have you been thoughtless in your judgments? If so, set about to correct them. If not, the Lord could have been chopping away at your pride or deepening your love by allowing you to love through an unlovely situation. Even if God does not show you why immediately, as you patiently and humbly wait totally resigned to Him, He will faithfully accomplish His work.

Just because God has placed your man in a position of leadership over you and directs you through him doesn't mean that he is any more important or superior as a person than you are. God chooses various ways to communicate—the object He uses is not the issue. Remember that God spoke to Balaam through his donkey. (See Num. 22.)

Gauge of Response to Others

One evidence of our success in relating to others as we relate to Jesus is shown by whether others offend us. Some years ago a houseguest made the comment during a conversation that one walking in the Spirit could not be offended. At first, I was taken back by the statement. However, as I pondered it and observed my own life, I saw the accuracy of the statement. When I am completely yielded to Jesus, my reaction to what others do and say is "I want to know the truth, Lord. Show me if I'm wrong. Teach me. I am available for You to use others in my life in any way You please."

By contrast, if I'm offended my attitude is often, "I am right and I will prove it." Or "You had no right to do or say that to me." One attitude is from the creature who is being taught by God, His Creator. The other is from a person trying to be his own god. "Great peace have they who love Your law; *nothing shall offend them* or make them stumble" (Ps. 119:165, AMP).

Are we grumblers, murmurers, and complainers? Do we have critical attitudes? Such actions carry with them a grave penalty. "Do not complain, brethren, against one another, so that you [yourselves] may not be judged" (James 5:9, AMP). To criticize another is really criticizing our Lord's workmanship and is not showing the reverence due His work.

Actually any attitudes of murmuring and complaining are very serious. So serious that in 40 years over 1 million Israelites died in the wilderness by God's judgment for their murmurings. We are to learn from the Israelites' mistakes. "We should not tempt the Lord . . . as some of them did . . . nor discontentedly complain as some of them

did. . . . These things befell them ¨as an example and warning''
(1 Cor. 10:9-11, AMP).

Open Ears Through Communication

The fact that God does lead us through our mates doesn't mean that we are not to communicate to them our needs, desires, and points of view. Instead that is part of our job as their helpmate. We see life from a different perspective than they do. Only when we share this added dimension do they have adequate information on which to make a good decision. However, care should be exercised in communicating, not to put down one's mate, condemn him, or appear as a know-it-all. This can be eliminated if you remember not to share on: (1) a man to man basis. For instance, ''I have it all worked out. This is the way to go about it.'' (2) Don't share in a motherly fashion either. (3) Don't ridicule. (4) Don't share from a pedestal like a wise old owl.

Instead say something like, ''Honey, I feel so and so'' or ''What would you think about such and such?'' When it involves the two of you personally concerning something he has done, instead of pointing an accusing finger at him, make yourself the problem. Say, for instance, ''I am having trouble knowing how to relate to you, or how I should handle my emotions at this time. Would you help me?''

Keep uppermost in your mind, that no matter how expertly you articulate, only Jesus opens ears giving understanding and oneness through communication. The following incident illustrates how easy it is to feel we have accomplished good communication only to be proven wrong.

Little Debbie enjoyed her daily telephone chat with her grandmother. But one morning her horrified mother watched her tiny lips pucker up accentuating her dimpled cheeks as she released these unexpected words. ''Gama, you ugie.''

Stammering a hurried apology, Mother hung up the receiver. Turning to her child, she talked with her for some time. Then she explained how to make an apology. Satisfied that Debbie understood, Mother called Gama back. ''Mother,'' she began, ''Debbie has something she wants to say to you.''

Taking the phone with confidence, Debbie apologized, ''Gama, I sorry you ugie.''

We smile as we imagine the young mother's dismay. For all her lecturing, she hadn't made herself clear. Yet Debbie thought she was obeying with her "apology." Likewise, we can think we are adequately communicating with our mates, and they may respond thinking they understand what we mean—yet they may never come close to hearing what we really said.

There was a time I thought DeWitt and I would never be able to communicate. Now it amazes me that we are reaching a oneness that often goes beyond words. Numerous times he or I will say something and the other responds with, "I was just fixing to say that same thing," or "That's exactly what I was thinking." That does not mean we always clearly communicate with each other. But now I know that the solution comes back to trusting Jesus to open ears and eyes. When He doesn't, it's because He is doing something much more important in me or in my husband.

Notes

[1] Paul Lee Tan, *Encyclopedia of 7700 Illustrations* (Rockville, MD: Assurance Publishers), p. 775.

[2] John D. Jess, *The Birds and the Bees* (Chicago: Moody Press), pp. 40-41.

10
Beholding Him Through Disillusionment

"It seems that I'm not getting better, but worse! It's so discouraging. I take one step forward and two backward."

"I get so disgusted and discouraged with myself. Just about the time I think I'm doing pretty good, I fall flat on my face."

"I get so tired of my failures. I know God must be totally disgusted with me. I'm so ashamed of myself."

"What kind of a witness do my failures make to the non-Christians around me? How could God possibly use me?"

Can you identify with any of these statements? Such feelings often arise from disillusionment. Our gracious, loving heavenly Father is liberating us to enjoy Him, ourselves, and others. To do so He must wipe away all of our false illusions about ourselves, others, and Himself. If we don't understand what is happening, the experience can be very frustrating.

Illusions of Self—I'm Nothing

It is easy to intellectually agree with God as we read verses which tell us that "nothing good dwells in me" (Rom. 7:18, NASB) and "apart from Me you can do nothing" (John 15:5). Yet it is quite another thing to experience these facts in our lives. Often when we do, we become discouraged. But we must recognize that such disillusionment is necessary for us to see the hopelessness of our situation apart from Christ and become helplessly dependent on Him.

God uses people and situations to allow us to see ourselves apart from Him. In the beginning of my intimate walk with Him, He used our small sons to begin wiping away my illusions about myself. I found myself being extremely impatient with them, going from one emotionally draining situation to another. There I was an adult— yelling and screaming as much or more than my three little preschool boys. How humiliating! Later, God used my husband to expose my helplessness apart from Him. And I know He will continue to use someone or something to wipe away any pride that should begin to creep in. Praise Him for His faithfulness!

In *The Practice of the Presence of God*,[1] Brother Lawrence's statement concerning his failures is so comforting to me. This godly man who lived in the 1600s wrote, "When I fail I simply admit my faults saying to God, 'I shall never do otherwise if You leave me to myself. It is You who must stop my falling and it is You who must amend that which is amiss.' "

Such an attitude as Brother Lawrence's is not one of irresponsibility. Instead it is one of reality. He is agreeing with Paul's words, "For it is *God who works in you to will and to act* according to His good purpose" (Phil. 2:13).

It is especially important to remember the truth of this verse when we are trying so hard to do right and really think we are succeeding. Then, without warning all falls apart and we are accused of doing something we weren't even aware we were doing. How discouraging! How can we not do something we don't know we're doing? What a helpless feeling. Indeed, even hopeless, if we forget that we're Jesus' responsibility. We remind the other person involved that no harm was intended. Then we turn to Jesus asking Him to do the life changing within because we are helpless to do any different if left to ourselves. As we behold Him, responding to Him in all that He shows us, His responsibility is to will in us and to act in us!

My Horribleness VS His Grace

As the great degree of our despicableness is revealed, to that degree we see the grace of our God. We truly begin to grasp what grace is—God's Riches At Christ's Expense. Truly, we can not help Him. Just as we couldn't help Him by entering into the blood covenant[2] that God made with us, through Christ's work on the cross. We simply behold Him, trust Him, and adhere to Him and He does the inward life-changing.

A friend fell to his knees and was crying out his unworthiness. "Lord, I have not had my quiet time now for two days. I haven't witnessed to one person this week concerning how to know You."

About halfway through his list, the Lord stopped him with the thought, "Son, your reasoning is saying to Me that you would be worthy of My blessing if you had done all of those things. You are missing the whole point. You are worthy to come into My presence in prayer and walk in My presence in fellowship daily, not because of what you do, but because of what Christ has done for you. You are worthy only because you are in Him!"

I believe one reason our Lord shows us how contemptible we are, is to allow us to see how gloriously magnificent and lovingly gracious He is. We truly cannot appreciate Him as we should till we see ourselves for what we really are without Him.

Relax—No Straining or Striving

"But," we might say, "I'm a new creature in Christ. Why isn't more of that showing?" The new person we are in Christ has to mature and that takes TIME. In the meantime, God uses our maturing process to increase our love for Him as He wipes away our prideful illusions of ourselves. Truly God wastes nothing. His plan is perfect.

Should you start wondering if you have grown at all or feel you have not, know by faith you have. Growing up in Him is Christ's responsibility as you cooperate with Him through obedience (Phil. 2:12-13). You can be sure He is not neglecting His job. Besides, you won't see yourself grow spiritually any more than you will physically.

The fact that we now see our sins shows real improvement. There was a time when we did not see what we were doing wrong. Only others and God saw and were aware of what a mess we were. Since God knew all our faults billions of years ago and made complete provision, He is never shocked or surprised by our failures. He never tires of our coming to Him for cleansing. Instead He is pleased because that is what Jesus died to provide.

So even if after taking one step forward we seem to take two backward, that is better than three backward. The fact that we are more aware of our weaknesses is proof within itself that we are improving. The closer we get to Jesus, the Light, the more our dirt shows up.

Do not draw back thinking, *Who needs that? Maybe it's not so great to live closer and closer to Him*. Never believe that lie. Drawing closer to God liberates us from trying to be something we are not. As He shows us what we are not, He at the same time shows us that He will always be what we need in an overflowing abundance. So even though it may be painful to see ourselves, it is a healthy pain—one that leads to real freedom from false illusions about ourselves.

Eliminating all illusions about ourselves takes out the straining and striving that often accompanies Christians' lives who feel they must produce their own holiness. Holiness is produced in us by Jesus as we simply behold Him and fellowship with Him. God is the one who makes us holy. *"Both the one who makes men holy* and those who are made holy are of the same family. So Jesus is not ashamed to call them brothers" (Heb. 2:11).

Straining to achieve the degree of maturity we see in another, can be discouraging—especially if we are trying to bring it about rather than relaxing in God as He matures us. The different books available on Madame Guyon's life,[3] a godly woman who lived in the 1600s, have had a tremendous influence on my life. I have been encouraged by the fact that regardless of the many hardships she suffered, each served only to increase her joy in the Lord.

However, at times I would read about levels of maturity that she had achieved which were so far from my level of growth that I would be discouraged. Then I'd simply back off and say, "God, I am Your responsibility. If I ever arrive to such areas of maturity, You will have to accomplish it. I can't!"

Even Paul wrote, "Not that I have already obtained all this, or have already been made perfect, but I press on to take hold of that for which Christ Jesus took hold of me" (Phil. 3:12).

Learning to relax in God—allowing Him to do His will in us without striving and straining to help Him out—takes time, especially if we want to achieve the right balance. St. Augustine's remark, *"Love God* and do as you please" speaks to the issue for me. Just keep the sequence as he states it, and there will be no problem.

One Day at a Time

To regularly experience God's overflowing joy, we must not try to solve this afternoon's problems this morning or tomorrow's problems today. "So do not worry or be anxious about tomorrow, for tomorrow will have worries and anxieties of its own. Sufficient for each day is its own trouble" (Matt. 6:34, AMP). Many of our problems are only in our minds and never happen anyway. Our Lord simply won't give us strength for problems in advance because that would be teaching us not to trust Him.

Sarah cried and cried one day over the phone asking how she would ever be able to bear more hurt and pain that she was anticipating. We carefully examined Matthew 6:34 together and gradually she sorted out things as they were, rather than as she anticipated. Two days later she called overflowing with joy. She had started beholding God, resting in His momenthby moment provision and He had comforted her heart. Jesus gave her insight into how He was working in the situation that had at first caused panic. We agreed that she should keep a notebook, writing out in detail the comfort and insights God had just given. Then, when her faith grew weak in the future, she could review His mighty works and be encouraged. Over and over God told Israel to "remember the wonders He has done" (Ps. 105:5). "But they soon forgot what He had done and did not wait for His counsel." (106:13).

During this time of pain, God also wiped away another one of Sarah's illusions. She had been crying out to Him, "Lord, I want to *know You*. I want that more than anything!" All the time she expected some big event to take place whereby she would then be able to say, "I now know You."

Instead God showed her that knowing Him was a gradual process. Simply by trusting and beholding Him moment by moment—one day at a time—Sarah was coming to know Him. When Jesus lets us see the hideousness of ourselves, He will at the same time let us see and *know* the wonder and all-sufficiency of Himself.

My Testimony?

Don't our mistakes keep us from giving an effective testimony to others? No. If we handle them properly, they will do just the reverse. When we become Christians, God doesn't "zap" us and make us instantly, experientially perfect. If another person only sees perfection in us and he becomes a Christian and fails, he might conclude: *I guess my Christianity did not take*. But if he sees us failing, admitting our faults, making the proper restitutions necessary, and walking on with God, then he'll know what to do when he fails. He will know that Christians are not perfect, but simply in the process of becoming more like God each day.

Illusions of Role

False illusions as to what constitutes an important role in life, especially for women, can be very damaging. The ERA movement in our country has done untold damage by implying that a woman is not really fulfilled or accomplishing things of importance unless she is pursuing a career. The implication is that only dummies stay home.

Often the church unintentionally contributes from a different angle to this erroneous view. Implications are made that one is not a dedicated Christian if they have not done X number of things at church, served on various committees, taught so many classes, or won so many to Christ. Sometimes in giving foreign or home missionaries the emphasis they deserve, those who are called to minister at home feel their role is less important. Of course, reverence, respect, and complete support must be given to fellow Christians God has called to serve in this very sacred and special way. At all times we are to be sensitive and available to God's leading to serve in various capacities in our church, to win others to Christ, and be ready to go to any mission field should He so ordain. We should not minimize the importance of such godly activities, but we should emphasize that which has been neglected—the value of the woman's role in the home.

Not to fulfill our God-given roles as wives and mothers is to bring reproach on His Word. Wives are to be self-controlled, pure, kind, busy at home, and "subject to their husbands, so that no one will malign the Word of God" (Titus 2:5). When we see the importance of the woman's role in the home, we will never again drop our heads and mumble apologetically, "I'm just a housewife," when asked what we do. We will realize that the home is the foundation of a stable society, and we are the heart of that home.

Illusions of Others

Having false illusions about ourselves torn down can be devastating if we don't realize what God is doing. Having our false illusions of others eliminated can be devastating too. How very easy it is to put others on a pedestal without realizing what we are doing till they come tumbling down and we are disappointed. Many Christians have been disillusioned by expecting perfection from other Christians and when they failed miserably, had their faith in Christianity sorely tested. The problem comes when we focus on others rather than Jesus.

We must learn from Jesus how to handle such disillusioning. Our Lord trusted no man; yet He was never suspicious, never bitter, never in despair about any man. He saw men and women as they were. Yet He made no stinging bitter remarks about them.[4] "Jesus would not entrust Himself to them . . . for He knew what was in man" (John 2:24-25). "For from within, out of men's hearts come evil thoughts, sexual immorality, theft, murder, adultery, greed, malice, deceit, lewdness, envy, slander, arrogance and folly" (Mark 7:21-22).

Jesus never expected perfection from people. Perfection only comes from the Father. He beheld the Father through each person, knowing what His grace could do for any man was so perfect that He despaired of no one. He beheld the Father instead of men and so must we.

The first time such disillusionment struck me forcibly was in the beginning of our evangelistic endeavors in the late 1960s. DeWitt and I were working with a pastor we trusted and respected. As we were planning to evangelize our community, we discovered our view of evangelism differed totally from the pastor's. I had expected opposition but not from other Christians. As I held my aching, questioning heart up to Jesus asking, "Why?" He clearly answered me. "Darien, please learn now that none of My children are perfect—just as you aren't. Keep your eyes on only Me and work with your co-workers with as much peace as possible. But do not put another Christian on a pedestal, or you will always be disappointed."

Another time I was horrified to hear I had been put on a pedestal. One summer about a year after I had stopped teaching my seminar on marriage, a lady wrote saying she was teaching my series to women in her town several hundred miles away. However, they had heard

DeWitt and I were divorced. She felt if this were true, it would discredit all the truths I had set forth. I was not totally surprised because about three months earlier a woman in our area called saying she had attended a class I had taught and after hearing the rumor of our divorce, simply had to know the truth. I thanked her for calling and appointed her to tell everyone she saw that we were happily married.

Of course, I reassured the other woman that we were happily married, also. But I challenged her that what God's Word said was the basis for any credibility, not whether a teacher or author applied it in his life. My prayer was that the entire class would learn through the incident to always look to Jesus, not to others. If this lesson was learned, it was well worth the misunderstanding.

Not only are we not to put an individual on a pedestal, but we are not to set a group or church apart, feeling that they and they alone have all the truth. God does not give all His revelation at any time to any one person or group. That means just as no person is perfect, so no gathering of people within a church or denominational group is perfect or has total revelation. All of us have some insight but still have areas in which to learn.

Knowing this, we can learn from others that which Christ has taught them, and share what He has taught us. That keeps us beholding Him, embracing what He shows us He would have us receive from others, without condemning them in the areas in which we differ (Phil. 3:15-16).

Illusions of Loved Ones

Illusions concerning our mates are often the hardest to turn loose. A comment from Alice Chapin's book, *500 Creative Ways to Say I LOVE YOU to the Man in Your Life*,[5] speaks directly to this point. "Remember there is only one kind of man to marry—a sinner. If I remarried I would have to adjust to some new sinner's set of faults."

As God removes our illusions concerning our mates, we might conclude, "I have fallen out of love with my husband," if we don't understand what God is doing or if we don't know what real love is.

We do not fall out of love. What happens is we stop releasing our love to an individual and the emotions of love die away. We choose whom we love. Much of our thinking today is governed by Hollywood's concept of love, rather than real love as God describes it. Hollywood love or psuedo love usually describes only the romantic feelings, such as the physical chemistry. When the bells stop ringing or the tingling stops, we conclude that love is gone. But true love is giving of yourself to meet another's needs without consideration of what you will receive in return.

God's Word describes real love. "Love endures long and is patient and kind; love never is envious nor boils over with jealousy; is not boastful or vainglorious, does not display itself haughtily. It is not conceited—arrogant and inflated with pride; it is not rude [unmannerly], and does not act unbecomingly. Love does not insist on its own rights or its own way, for it is not self-seeking; it is not touchy or fretful or resentful; it takes no account of the evil done to it—pays no attention to a suffered wrong. It does not rejoice at injustice and unrighteousness, but rejoices when right and truth prevail. Love bears up under anything and everything that comes, is ever ready to believe the best of every person, its hopes are fadeless under all circumstances and it endures everything" (1 Cor. 13:4-7, AMP).

Reread this passage and replace the word *love* with *Jesus*. Then read it again, replacing the word *love* with your name. Lastly, read it substituting the words, *Jesus within me*, for *love*. Once we have done this, we begin to see what real love is. We see how we must cooperate with Jesus for Him to accomplish such love within us and through us.

Most of us could identify with Sarah when she said, "I can see I have never really loved. I have wanted to possess or to get. But love is giving of yourself without any regard for getting in return."

As we by faith release love to our mates regardless of our feelings, God will eventually rekindle the emotions of love that may not presently be there. Matthew 6:21 reminds us that where your treasure is, there will your heart be also. Begin today treasuring your mate and releasing your love toward him through loving words and loving actions.

Illusions About God

Just as our illusions of self and others must be removed, so must our illusions about God. If we predetermine in our little minds a set of pat answers or formulas as to how God will work, we are sure to be disillusioned. Isaiah 55:9 tells us, "As the heavens are higher than the earth, so are My ways higher than your ways and My thoughts than your thoughts."

Elaine had concluded that if she did everything she could as a wife, God would not allow her marriage with Tom to end. When it did, she was left wondering why. Others in a similar situation could blame God, feeling He had failed them when things did not happen as they had expected they would. Their faith in God could then be sorely shaken.

We must release all conclusions we have about how God will work and realize that His ways reach beyond ours. "O the depth of the riches and wisdom and knowledge of God! How unfathomable [inscrutable, unsearchable] are His judgments—His decisions! And how untraceable [mysterious, undiscoverable] are His ways—His methods, His paths!" (Rom. 11:33, AMP) Only when we defer to His judgments giving Him complete liberty to be our God will we not be offended by His ways. "Blessed . . . is he who takes no offense in Me and who is not hurt or resentful or annoyed or repelled or made to stumble, [whatever may occur]" (Luke 7:23, AMP).

Our Lord may work in our lives using traditionally expected means, or He may work totally opposite to anything we would expect. I find the latter in my life most often. This keeps me ever mindful that He is God, and I am the creature.

At certain times of our lives, God often gives miraculous instantaneous answers to prayer and needs. Other times we see no visible results. Sometimes we are not aware of His presence, and other times we are aware of His presence. At one point He may lead us in one direction, then later lead us in a totally different direction. Regardless of His dealings with us, we must not attempt to second guess God or even figure Him out. We must say with the psalmist, "As for God, His way is perfect; the Word of the Lord is flawless. He is a shield for all who take refuge in Him" (Ps. 18:30).

Notes

[1] Brother Lawrence, *The Practice of the Presence of God* (Old Tappan, NJ: Spire Books).

[2] Review this concept in Chapter 3.

[3] Madame Guyon, *Madame Guyon: An Autobiography* (Chicago: Moody Press).

T.C. Upham, *The Life of Madame Guyon* (Greenwood, SC: The Attic Press, Inc.).

Jeanne Guyon, *Experiencing the Depths of Jesus Christ* (Goleta, CA: Christian Books).

[4] Oswald Chambers, *My Utmost for His Highest* (Toronto: McClelland & Stewart Limited), pp. 152, 212.

[5] Alice Chapin, *500 Creative Ways to Say I LOVE YOU to the Man in Your Life* (Buchanan, GA: His Way Library).

11
Beholding Him Through Temptation and Suffering

One important key in beholding our God is learning to see Him through the temptations and sufferings that bombard us. What do you do with those wrong or negative thoughts that keep recurring? How do you keep from reliving an unpleasant situation or a dreaded anticipated scene in the theater of your mind?

Temptation VS Sin

First of all, temptation itself is not sin. For a thought to walk across your mind is not sin. However, how you deal with that thought can determine whether or not it does become sin. "Each one is tempted when, by his own evil desire, he is dragged away and enticed. Then, after desire has conceived, it gives birth to sin; and sin, when it is full-grown, gives birth to death" (James 1:14-15).

For instance, you and your husband are at a gathering and you catch a smile he exchanged with an attractive woman next to him. Immediately your area of weakness, jealousy, rises to its tiptoes and your imagination goes wild. The thought walks across your mind, *Is he interested in her in an unwholesome way? Perhaps, they have met and become involved on previous occasions or something is about to begin between the two.*

Or consider the reverse situation. Your husband has not been understanding or affectionate and you catch the eye of a man across the room, who is attractive to you, and he gives you a warm, inviting smile. You think, *He seems so much nicer than my husband. How wonderful it would be to have him wrap me in his understanding and comfort me in his arms.*

So far, no sin has happened within your mind. But the next step can determine whether it does. If you allow such a thought to drag you away and entice you, it will become sin. It is like sitting down with the thought to entertain it and embrace it. Once that happens, the desire is conceived and gives birth to sin. In these cases the sin would be jealousy or adultery. The sin of adultery begins with giving your affections and loyalty to another whether literally or mentally.

Handling Temptation

What does one do with wrong or potentially wrong thoughts? Whether the thought is one which could lead to jealousy, adultery, or mistrust of God and His love for us, we do not gain release from it by trying not to think about it. In struggling directly with the thought, thinking, *I will not think that thought again*, you've then thought about it twice as much as before you started struggling with it. Such an approach only strengthens the temptation. Temptation resisted in this fashion only ends in our being wounded or totally defeated.

In the face of temptation, we must immediately recognize our helplessness to conquer it and turn to Jesus. By doing so, we claim and recognize the truth set forth by Paul. "The weapons we fight with are not the weapons of the world. On the contrary, they have divine power to demolish strongholds. We demolish arguments and every pretension that sets itself up against the knowledge of God, and *we take captive every thought to make it obedient to Christ* (2 Cor. 10:4-5). In turning to Jesus we claim the victory He provided for us on the cross. We turn the thought over to Him as His prisoner, allowing Him to lead it off as a bound, gagged, and chained captive.

By reacting immediately to such wrong thoughts, we don't give the enemy a chance to get a foothold in our lives. God's Word tells us to deal quickly with sin. In the Book of Ephesians, Paul pinpoints sinful anger. "Do not let the sun go down while you are still angry, and do not give the devil a foothold" (Eph. 4:26-27). The longer we play with temptation the greater foothold the enemy gains in our lives.

Instead of struggling directly with the temptation itself, we should respond as a little child that perceives a monster. He does not stand there and try to fight the thing. He will, in fact, hardly look at it. He quickly shrinks into his mother's arms in complete confidence of safety. Likewise, we should turn from the dangers of temptation to God by casting ourselves into His presence. Such was the course that David took according to Psalm 16:8-9. "I have set the Lord always before me. Because He is at my right hand, I will not be shaken. Therefore, my heart is glad and my tongue rejoices; my body also will rest secure."

As we cast ourselves into God's presence, we *replace* the wrong thought rather than struggle with it. We replace it with thoughts of our loving, holy God—who He is and what He has and is doing in our lives. "Whatever is true, whatever is noble, whatever is right, whatever is pure, whatever is lovely, whatever is admirable—if anything is excellent or praiseworthy—think about such things" (Phil. 4:8).

Dwelling on temptation is not the way to have victory, but it is the way the enemy tries to keep us from beholding our God. Kelly was excited as she shared how God had shown her this. One day as she was wrestling with dieting and thoughts of food, God showed her that she was giving all her thoughts and affections to food rather than Him. How subtle our enemy is. He will use anything to break up that vital and crucial relationship that comes as a result of beholding our God.

Breaking Down Footholds

All of us have areas of weakness that result from our wrong habits or wrong thought processes. These may be there because of footholds we have given the enemy by not promptly dealing with temptation. Or they may be there simply because certain areas of our lives have not yet been conformed to Christ's image. Regardless, they are well-formed and will take longer to work through. Occasionally, our Lord will instantly deliver us from a habit or sin that enslaves us. But usually He allows us to learn discipline and dependency on Him as we gradually retrain our thoughts and actions.

One such example was my mother's problem with food. Not only had she not been trained in eating healthy foods, but she had exaggerated the importance of food. She sought to solve her various problems by eating. After she committed her eating problem to the Lord, He took her through many phases of teaching before she saw ultimate victory. First, she learned under the care of a nutritionist how to eat healthfully. After she had success in this area, the Lord showed her that to bring her eating habits initally under control she would need a strict healthy diet in which she was regularly accountable to others.

Through such a program her body was assured of getting the necessary nutrients, thereby eliminating her body's abnormal cravings caused by improper nourishment. She realized that eating when she didn't need to was a reaction to anxiety.

Through such a plan of commitment, she arrived at her desired weight, and as the controls of her diet were lessened, she learned to exercise the needed restraints while in a supervised atmosphere. Victory is now realized. However, she knows she will probably always have to set up guidelines for herself in this area of weakness.

In the case of ingrained habits or strong weaknesses, a plan of action must often be formed and carried out while remaining in total dependency on the Lord. Until we can become strong enough in the Lord, we often need the help of others and/or the avoidance of the temptation until a level of maturity or resistance is achieved in this area.

Suffering Refines and Purifies

Just as temptations draw us closer to God and strengthen us in Him so does suffering—whether it is suffering that applies to our souls or to our bodies.

God uses suffering to purify and refine us. (Note that the suffering referred to here is not as a result of direct, willful disobedience. However, even that kind of suffering is designed by God for our blessing, because He uses it to bring us to repentance and ultimate blessing.)

The penalty for sin has been paid so there is no condemnation, but sin has corrupted our nature so it must be purged. Since our God is a refiner, He says, "I have tested you in the furnace of affliction" (Isa. 48:10). The furnace referred to is the kind used to refine gold and silver. Such a furnace was used for separation. God is separating us to Himself in much the same way as the dross is separated from gold and silver through the heat of the refining furnace.

God says, "I will turn My hand upon thee (KJV), I will thoroughly purge away your dross and remove your impurities (Isa. 1:25). Our God brings about such suffering out of love because He knows this is the only way to empty us of certain impurities so that we may offer to Him an offering in righteousness. "He will sit as a refiner and purifier of silver; He will purify the Levites and refine them like gold and silver. Then the Lord will have men who will bring offerings in righteousness" (Mal. 3:3).

When suffering comes, even though we do not know the reason, we should respond as Job, "He knoweth the way that I take; when He hath tried me, I shall come forth as gold" (Job 23:10, KJV). We know that God loves us and is getting us ready to be Jesus' bride for eternity. Whatever it takes to make us ready we must embrace.

When we examine the value that refining, purifying, and separation has to steel, we begin to grasp how important God's purifying of us is. It is said that a bar of steel worth $5, when made into ordinary horseshoes will be worth only $10. If this same $5 bar is manufactured into needles, its value rises to $350. But if it is made into delicate springs for expensive watches, it will be worth $250,000. This original bar of steel is made more valuable by being cut to its proper size, passed through the heat again and again, hammered and manipulated, beaten and pounded, finished and polished till it is finally ready for its delicate task.

Be comforted—God expends His efforts only on that which gives promise of having value. Your suffering proves God's love for you. He desires to bless you as you receive it from Him and behold Him through it.

Suffering Humbles

Suffering has a way of humbling us as nothing else can. It reminds us that we are the creatures totally dependent on our Creator.

Jesus said, "Unless a kernel of wheat falls to the ground and dies, it remains only a single seed. But if it dies, it produces many seeds" (John 12:24). This is the law of life in the natural realm, and it is the law of life in the spiritual sphere also. There is no making without breaking. Someone has accurately stated "There is no gain without pain."

Suffering is a valuable tool in our Lord's hands. Our Lord encouraged me a year or so ago as I shared with Pat Bradley, who helped me with my first book. Because of a move, we had not been together for years. As we reminisced, I shared some of my suffering—especially in the years since I had stopped teaching. Pat concluded, "Darien, I can see the fruits of that suffering. The only way I know to describe it is that you have become tenderized in much the same way meat becomes tender under the heat from a pressure cooker."

Often, we cannot see what needs to be broken in us. I had not seen within myself what Pat had seen. However, such humbling often can be accomplished only through suffering. My sister was visiting my home when an incident occurred that hurt me deeply. When I could contain it no longer, I cried out my hurt before her. As we examined it together, she concluded, "Darien, there seems to be no explanation as to why. God just must have known that you needed to hurt." Praise His name that He is faithful and we can trust Him to do whatever is necessary to break us so that we give forth a fragrance that is a delight to Him.

The psalmist writes, "You do not delight in sacrifice, or I would bring it; You do not take pleasure in burnt offerings. The sacrifices of God are a broken spirit; a broken and contrite heart, O God, You will not despise" (Ps. 51:16-17). For years my prayer has been that God would bring about a broken and contrite spirit within me. As I searched for ways that I could cooperate with Him so that He could release His overflowing joy within me, He led me to the writings of William Law. Law says, "If you ask what this one, true, simple, plain, immediate, and unerring way is, it is the way of patience, meekness, humility, and resignation to God." [1]

My heart rejoiced with Law's explanation, but my questioning mind yearned to have this amplified. God answered my request through Andrew Murray's commentary on Law's statement. To embrace each circumstance with patience, meekness, humility, and resignation means responding to each circumstance thusly: (1) "at once gently sink down before God in a humility that confesses its nothingness; (2) in the meekness that bows under and quietly bears the shame we feel; (3) in a patience that waits God's sure deliverance; and (4) a resignation that gives itself entirely to His will, and power, and mercy." [2]

Obedience Through Suffering

Some have said, "But I don't know if I want to suffer." That simply is not the issue. We all live in a world contaminated with sin, and we will suffer. The issue is whether we will allow God to be glorified in and through us during our suffering. The same sun that hardens bricks also melts butter. If we properly receive the suffering that comes to us, He will use it to melt us into obedient children. When properly accepted, suffering blesses us and honors Him.

Just as God used suffering in our Lord's life to develop obedience, so will He in our lives. "Although He was a Son, He learned obedience from what He suffered" (Heb. 5:8). Then we read, "In bringing many sons to glory, it was fitting that God, for whom and through whom everything exists, should make the author of their salvation perfect through suffering" (2:10).

If God used suffering in our Lord's life, why shouldn't He do the same in ours? "I tell you the truth, no servant is greater than his master" (John 13:16).

God's use of suffering to purify us, break us, and produce obedience in us is just the beginning. There are many reasons for suffering. The following list suggests some other reasons:

1. Suffering brings us to salvation (2 Cor. 7:9-10).
2. Suffering enables us to glorify God. See John 11 which describes Lazarus' sickness, death, and being brought back to life.
3. Suffering makes us appreciative.
4. Suffering teaches us to depend on God.
5. Suffering makes us sympathetic to others during their suffering (2 Cor. 1:3-6).
6. Suffering silences Satan. (Read the Book of Job.)
7. Suffering teaches us to pray.
8. Suffering produces fruit (John 15:2).
9. Suffering produces perfection (1 Peter 5:10).
10. Suffering brings rewards (2 Tim. 2:12; 1 Peter 4:12-13).
11. Suffering prepares us to reign with Him (2 Tim. 2:12).

His Will Through Suffering

At all times we must allow God to be God in our sufferings. We should let Him use our pain according to His all wise purpose, rather than attempting to tell Him what to do. Since we are locked into the pages of time, we cannot see the overall story that God is writing in our lives. Our view of today's problems would be like limiting us to page 110 of our life's story. But our Lord is the author of our life's book and knows what to write on each page in order to make the ending come out for our advantage and His honor and glory. Therefore, we must not tell Him how and what to write, but submit to His master penmanship.

Dallas Holm discovered the blessing of allowing God to be God during his wife's bout with a rare, hereditary disease of the intestinal tract called Peutz-Jeghers syndrome. The doctors said that the polyps or tumors in Linda's small intestines had to be removed through surgery. None of it made sense. Linda and Dallas were living for the Lord, serving Him in a full-time ministry. Dallas was a crusade soloist with Dave Wilkerson. His best-selling record had hit the top of the Gospel music charts. They had a solid marriage and a great family.

The night before Linda's scheduled surgery, Dallas fell to his knees once again in a nearby motel. Even though the 75 people at Twin Oaks Ranch, where the families lived as a part of David Wilkerson's World Challenge ministry, had joined praying for her full healing, Dallas reasoned that maybe Linda hadn't been healed because he hadn't been specific enough. He poured out his heart telling God just how he felt, his fears for Linda through the surgery, and his concern for himself and their daughter should she die.

Dallas said, "What followed was amazing. I can't say I heard a voice. I don't know that I've ever heard the audible voice of the Lord, but I know He spoke to me that night."

"You have two choices," He seemed to be saying, "You can have your miracle if that's what you want. I can heal Linda tonight without surgery. Or, she can have the operation. There will be some pain. Her recovery will take about 10 days. But in the process, you will learn some things about each other, about yourselves, and about Me that you would never be able to learn any other way."

"The choice was obvious. If Linda could be healed with just a simple prayer request, of course that was what I wanted. But the still, small voice was insistent: 'If you take the easy way, you'll be missing a valuable experience.'"

After a struggle Dallas remembered, "The Scripture says we are all bought with a price. Our bodies don't belong to us; they belong to God. In that light, the decision was simple.

"Lord, I yield to You—to whatever You think is best for our lives. Our bodies are Yours. All that we have, all that we are belongs to You. I simply ask that You go through this experience with us. Let Your will be done."

During the next 10 days, Linda recovered at such a rapid rate the doctors were astounded. Dallas felt his wife had been given back to him—like a gift. Every minute together was new and precious. Life had never looked so good.

"The wisdom of the Lord began to shine through the dark clouds that had hovered over them so long. Linda's fear of the polyp-producing disease, which had gripped her since the day she learned it was hereditary, was gone! She was free!

"And Dallas learned for himself something about the ways of the Almighty. As others before him, he found that He doesn't always deliver us from painful situations. Like the three Hebrew boys who were cast into the fiery furnace, sometimes He delivers us through the ordeal. Such a discovery produced a new confidence in God." [3]

God is also using my health to teach me many valuable lessons that I am sure I couldn't learn any other way. I can be assured of that because God always chooses the least painful way to teach us what we must learn in order to be ready to be Jesus' bride for eternity.

My health was a contributing factor in my decision to stop teaching my marriage seminar. As I struggled with the problem I wondered—*Would God heal me directly, use doctors, or what?* As I came to the place of having difficulty even in meeting my family's physical needs, it was evident that God was not going to directly heal me. Some physical relief was obtained, but not enough for me to function at a comfortable capacity. I accepted the fact that my physical ability would be limited and began making the necessary adjustments.

Complete peace became mine in regard to my health. God is sovereign and to His care I trusted and placed my whole self—body, soul, and spirit. Shortly after that, He led me to a doctor whose specialty was circulation with a mode of treatment fashioned to deal with the uncommon condition that I wasn't even aware I had.

While spending a week in this doctor's clinic, God began teaching me the balance He wanted me to obtain in my life. He showed me that in my burning zeal to share His Good News with others and minister to them, I had abused my body which was very important to Him. My idea, without consciously realizing it, had been—*Why spend so much time caring for a body that is in the process of decaying and certainly won't last for eternity? I want to be totally caught up in "spiritual" things.*

My problem was just the opposite of my mother's. She practically lived to eat, and I ate and rested only when I was forced to. God showed me afresh that my body was His temple. My physical body was groaning with the rest of nature under the bondage of decay. As Paul wrote, "Not only so, but we ourselves, who have the firstfruits of the Spirit, groan inwardly as we wait eagerly for our adoption as sons, the redemption of our bodies" (Rom. 8:23). Until a new body is given to me, I saw that it is "spiritual" to take proper care of the one I have. It was through carrying out the mundane, ordinary chores needed in caring for my body that God could work effectively in my life. I needed such discipline and balance.

Not only am I learning to care for and live with my particular circulatory problem, but I am learning to give my body nutrients that are necessary for health—such as drinking 6—8 glasses of water daily, which certainly doesn't come naturally to me. I am learning to spend more time with food preparation, so that we can cut down on such things as white flour, refined sugar, and caffeine. The need for proper exercise became evident too. Though I thrived on activity, exercise had always seemed a waste of time.

God has also used my health problems to give me compassion for others' sufferings. Life is not as black and white or "cut and dried" as I would like for it to be. Through it all, God has become God. I am learning to be totally abandoned to Him.

God must show each person the balance they need. Mother had a time of adjustment when she learned the importance of eating healthfully. Only God can bring each of us into the balance He wants for our lives at any particular stage of growth. And only He can show us what is needed by us individually at the different stages of our maturity. He will show us if we ask. (See James 1:5.)

Maturing of Our Faith Through Suffering

The maturing of our faith is the crucial issue in suffering. However our Lord chooses to work, we are to praise His holy name. Paul E. Billheimer's books, *Destined for the Throne* and *Don't Waste Your Sorrows*, have greatly blessed my life. How grateful I am to him and his wife, Jenny, for allowing me to share some of what God has taught them in and through their suffering and how God uses it to mature our faith.

God miraculously healed Rev. Billheimer's tuberculosis when he was a young man. The Lord also granted him a wonderful healing ministry, without his putting special emphasis on this area, as part of his general ministry. The first major testing that the Lord took them through when He did not give them a miraculous, instantaneous healing was in his wife Jenny's life.

When their last child was born as a result of an emergency cesarean, the surgeon told Mrs. Billheimer to be back in six months for a hysterectomy because her uterus was a solid mass of fibroid tumors. Mrs. Billheimer said, "At that time we thought it would be a sin for us to have medical help in such a situation, that we should pray and get a direct healing from the Lord."

After eight years passed, she faced two very humiliating and embarrassing situations as a result of hemorrhaging. In her desperation and search for God's will, He communicated that she was to have surgery. God worked marvelously through each circumstance to reassure her that He was in complete control. She raised her heart to Him in thanksgiving for the beautiful work He did through the surgeon.

Later Mrs. Billheimer found it necessary to submit to surgery again because of a serious problem with infection in her right index finger. While in the hospital, the Lord called her attention to Hebrews 11:35, 39. "*But others* trusted God and were beaten to death. . . . And these men of faith, though they *trusted God and won His approval*, none of them received all that God had promised them" (LB). This opened up a whole new line of thought for the Billheimers. *We had not failed* if through this fiery testing time, our faith had held steady and *we had won God's approval*. It is not the method by which deliverance comes *but the triumph of our faith* such as Job expressed, "Though He slay me, yet will I trust in Him" (Job 13:15, KJV). That is more precious to God than gold that perisheth though it be by fire, is to us. *It is the maturing of our faith that wins God's approval.* Hallelujah!

Mrs. Billheimer shared that they did not have the answers as to why God heals instantaneously at times and other times chooses to use other means such as doctors. Just last year God chose to have Rev. Billheimer's vision restored through cataract surgery with a plastic lens implant.

She concludes, "God has His sovereign plans and I think there are some things that He tells us are none of our business. That is what He told Peter when he asked the Lord what He was going to have for John. "What is that to thee? Follow thou Me" (John 21:22, KJV). In everyday language, He was saying, "Peter, that is none of your business. You just do what I tell you to do and leave John to Me."

"There are times," Mrs. Billheimer continued, "when I have felt that the Lord told me that the reason why was none of my business. I cannot explain a lot of things in our lives." How beautiful their testimony is to me. Such an attitude keeps God in His rightful place in our lives and us in total submission to Him.

Embrace Without Resistance

Since God uses suffering in our lives to purify us, break us, and develop obedience as well as for many other reasons, we should embrace it, allowing Him to complete His work as quickly as possible. This means that we simply allow the hurt to hurt as we behold Him, rather than trying to divert our attention or change our circumstances.

Sarah and I discussed this one day as she was attempting to escape her problems. At one point in time she was considering getting a job outside of the home and at another time she simply was going to divert her attention through shopping. Neither of these things, if done for the right reasons, is wrong. But in Sarah's case, she was considering them to avoid dealing with a problem God had before her. She had to learn the lesson of embracing her hurt and allowing God to "pull it out of her"—just as my mother learned this lesson through some hurts in her life.

Mother's evaluation of how to successfully deal with pain has been very valuable to me. She said, "In the past I felt like running away from the hurt. I am now learning that I am not to run away or fight, but to just sit and hurt. In doing so, I am opening up the gaping wound to the Lord and letting Him comfort and heal from the inside out— instead of putting a Band-Aid on the infected area." (By the way, there must be no self-pity involved.)

Mother compares our hurts being relieved in this way to childbirth. If one fights against the pain, it increases. If one does not resist the pains as they come but pushes along with them, it doesn't hurt nearly as bad. The birth is then brought about as painlessly as possible. The pain is used to bring forth the birth. Likewise, we are not to resist the hurt God allows in our lives, but submit to Him and let Him take care of it. When it is finally healed by Him, there are no scars such as come from "running from it" or resisting His working.

As I embrace pain it helps me (1) to appreciate my Lord even more. I remember that He hates sin. That is why He gave His life to gain the victory over sin for us. (2) I then want to cooperate with Him in order to turn loose of any known sin through confession, as well as submit to Him as He empties me of all impurities. (3) I, in turn, begin to develop a real distaste for sin and the ravaging effects it has on me, as I know my Lord hates sin with a holy wrath.

Limits to Suffering

Our compassionate, loving Father puts limits on our suffering. We can be assured it will not last forever. "Grain must be ground to make bread; so one does not go on threshing it forever" (Isa. 28:28). So it is with our lives. The psalmist writes, "Sing to the Lord, you saints of His; praise His holy name. For His anger lasts only a moment, but His favor lasts a lifetime; weeping may remain for a night, but rejoicing comes in the morning" (Ps. 30:4-5).

God will never give us more than we can stand as we keep our eyes on Him. God not only sets the limits, but He regulates the size and time of our suffering. (See 2 Cor. 12:9 and 1 Cor. 10:13.) At times we may feel it is almost too much as my sister Jan expressed after I helped her work through a problem. Her thanks came to me in a note on my birthday. She said, "Happy Birthday, Sis. I'm glad you were born so you could help me learn to die! Now we know why there are eight years between us. I couldn't have 'taken' this 'overflowing joy' any sooner!! I love you.''

Accompaniment and Deliverance Through Suffering

Our Lord accompanies us through our sufferings. He does not stand across the valley of pain beckoning us to hurry on through to join Him on the mountain of ease. We know He goes through it all with us because He lives within us through the Spirit and we are joined to Him by the blood covenant. (See chapter 3.) Whatever happens to us happens to Him also. ''For we do not have a High Priest who is unable to understand and sympathize and have a fellow feeling with our weaknesses and infirmities'' (Heb. 4:15, AMP).

David was aware of his Lord's careful attention to each and every one of his hurts. In Psalm 56:8, he expressed it this way. ''You number and record my wanderings; *put my tears into Your bottle*; are they not in Your book?'' (AMP)

We are not always aware of how tenderly He is sustaining us, but we can know that He is. The following story is a comforting reminder of His care for us in times of trial. One night a man had a dream. He dreamed he was walking along the beach with the Lord. Across the sky flashed scenes from his life. After each scene, he noticed two sets of footprints in the sand: one belonging to him, and the other to the Lord.

When the last scene of his life flashed before him, he looked back at the footprints in the sand. He noticed that many times there was only one set of footprints. He also noticed that it happened at the very lowest and saddest times in his life.

This really bothered him, and he questioned the Lord about it. ''Lord, You said that once I decided to follow You, You would walk with me all the way. But I have noticed that during the most troublesome times in my life, there is only one set of footprints. I don't understand why when I needed You most, You left me.''

The Lord replied, ''My son, My precious child, I love you and I would never leave you. During your times of trial and suffering, when you see only one set of footprints, it was then I carried you.''

So during those times when the hurt is so deep and God seems so distant, rest in His arms knowing that He is indeed sustaining and delivering you through it. Such is the Lord's promise. "The righteous cry out, and the Lord hears them; He delivers them from all their troubles. The Lord is close to the brokenhearted and saves those who are crushed in spirit. A righteous man may have many troubles, but the Lord delivers him from them all" (Ps. 34:17-19).

Notes

[1] William Law, edited by Andrew Murray, *Freedom From a Self-Centered Life/Dying to Self* (Minneapolis: Bethany Fellowship), p. 75.

[2] *Ibid.*, p. 79.

[3] Dallas Holm with Robert Paul Lamb, "I've Never Seen the Righteous Forsaken," *Charisma*, July/August 1980, pp. 23-25.

12
Beholding
Him Through Praise

Praise the Lord! Hallelujah!
Praise the Lord, O my soul!
While I live will I praise the Lord.
I will sing praises to my God
while I have any being.
The Lord shall reign forever,
Even Your God, O Zion, from generation to generation.
Praise the Lord! Hallelujah! (Ps. 146:1-2, 10, AMP)

Upon arising in the mornings do you lift up your soul to God in praise as Psalm 146 says? Is your day laced with such praise as you think thoughts and perform activities? Is the last thought that walks across your mind and slips through your lips before drifting off to sleep at night that of praise and adoration for your life of the day—the Lord Jesus Christ?

Living in Father's House

If not, consider embracing such a life. "But why should I?" you might ask. Because our desire is to live in a oneness with our Lord in His presence. Our God dwells in an atmosphere of praise. Even though God is omnipresent, He is especially present in the praises of His children. "But Thou art holy, O Thou that inhabitest the praises of Israel" (Ps. 22:3, KJV). Where there is adoration, reverence, and acceptable worship and praise, there our God identifies and manifests His presence. Praise and His presence have a mutual affinity.

Not only do we want to live in a conscious awareness of His presence daily, but we are getting ready to live in our Father's house forever. Jesus said, ''In My Father's house are many rooms; if it were not so, I would have told you. I am going there to prepare a place for you. And if I go to prepare a place for you, I will come back and take you to be with Me that you also may be where I am'' (John 14:2-3).

Most of us enjoy house guests from time to time. Have you ever noticed a pattern that sometimes develops? The first day there is nonstop talk and exuberant joy over renewing past acquaintances. Then as the days wear on, the exuberance begins to die down and you are found saying, ''When is´it that your plane leaves?'' or ''How much longer will you be able to stay with us?'' It is not that you do not love the persons visiting you, but your ways are different. Adjustments and concessions have to be made while they are there in order to keep things running smoothly. If the hardships and tensions are to be relieved, your ways and thinking would need to mesh into one. Likewise, for us to live in our Father's house forever such a meshing is necessary.

Considering that our Lord changes not and is the ''same yesterday and today and forever'' (Heb. 13:8), guess who is going to change? Right—you and me!

Looking into the activities of our Father's house, we see that praise is one of the chief occupations of angels. ''I saw the Lord seated on a throne, high and exalted. . . . Above Him were seraphs. . . . And they were calling to one another: 'Holy, holy, holy is the Lord Almighty; the whole earth is full of His glory' '' (Isa. 6:1-3).

As Jesus opened up the windows of heaven, He allowed John to observe similar activities. ''Then I looked and heard the voice of many angels, numbering thousands upon thousands, and ten thousand times ten thousand. They encircled the throne and the living creatures and the elders. In a loud voice they sang: 'Worthy is the Lamb, who was slain, to receive power and wealth and wisdom and strength and honor and glory and praise!' '' (Rev. 5:11-12) ''Then I heard what sounded like a great multitude, like the roar of rushing waters and like loud peals of thunder, shouting: 'Hallelujah! For our Lord God Almighty reigns. Let us rejoice and be glad and give Him glory!' '' (19:6-7)

Importance of Praise

Praise is important to our God. All of us are aware of the importance of prayer, yet there is more emphasis in the Bible on praise than on prayer. Upon examination of the major teachings emphasized by churches, none occupy the place of prominence in the Scriptures that praise does. The second coming of Christ is mentioned 318 times. Repentance is spoken of 110 times. Sanctification—72 times and justification—70 times, while the virgin birth is mentioned only twice. Yet praise is taught 332 times along with its first cousins of rejoicing and thanksgiving, each 288 times and 135 times respectively.

Praise easily outranks all the other major teachings. Then, if we added the references to praise, rejoicing, and thanksgiving, we would get a total of 755 references. The evidence is conclusive. Praise is extremely important!

Praise and thanksgiving can easily be combined because of their similarities and areas of overlapping. Each is an expression to God of gratefulness as we recognize and bow in submission to His sovereignty. However, thanksgiving seems to be directed more toward what is happening to me, whereas praise is directed to God for who He is and what He has done. Praise and rejoicing are often interchanged as well.

Praise—Appropriate Response

Praising God is to be the natural response of all of God's creation. "All Your works shall praise You, O Lord" (Ps. 145:10, AMP). Psalm 148 points out that the angels, the sun and moon, all the stars of light, the sea animals, the elements, the beasts, cattle, creeping and flying birds as well as the mountains, hills, and trees are to praise God. How do they do that? By living and functioning as they are programmed by our God. The jonquils in my yard are praising the Lord by opening up their beautiful blooms. The waters praise the Lord by staying within the bounds God set for them.

What about us, God's next of kin? "You are a chosen people, . . . a people belonging to God, *that you may declare the praises of Him* who called you out of darkness into His wonderful light" (1 Peter 2:9). We, of all of His creation, are to be praisers of God. Psalm 33:1

reminds us that praise is appropriate for God's children. "Rejoice in the Lord, O you righteous, for *praise is becoming and appropriate* for those who are upright in heart!" (AMP) Not only is it appropriate for us to praise our God, it was for this purpose we were created. "This people have I formed for Myself; they shall show forth My praise" (Isa. 43:21, KJV).

It follows that the highest of God's creation, man, was hit the hardest by sin and therefore has the hardest time being restored to the highest occupation in life—that of praising God. Our enemy will do anything to keep us from praising and worshipping God because praise from men, His children, means so much to God. Not only is it glorifying to God, but it lifts and blesses us beyond any other activity. Therefore, Jesus came to break the bands that bind our souls and bodies in despair and defeat so that we can be lifted up to Him in praise. He was sent "to proclaim freedom for the captives and release for the prisoners, . . . to bestow . . . a garment of praise instead of a spirit of despair" (Isa. 61:1, 3).

Our God is worthy of praise. "Let them praise and exalt the name of the Lord, for His name alone is exalted and supreme! His glory and majesty are above earth and heaven!" (Ps. 148:13, AMP) "Worthy are You, our Lord and God, to receive the glory and honor and dominion, for You created all things; by Your will they were [brought into being] and were created" (Rev. 4:11, AMP). Not only is He worthy of praise, but this praise should be given to Him by His children. "Your loving ones shall *bless You*—affectionately and gratefully shall Your saints confess and *praise* You!" (Ps. 145:10, AMP)

Somehow our praises minister to God. Because we know He delights in our fellowshipping with Him, could it be that He enjoys our praise in much the same way we enjoy our children's admiration and praise? What an honor to be able to minister to our Lord in this way.

When we praise or bless God, we are actually returning His love to Him. Such makes a sweet fragrance to God comparable to the incense burned by the priests of Israel in the holy place before entering into God's presence—the holy of holies.

We might even compare our praising and blessing God, and I speak most reverently, to giving a "party" for God. We stand and applaud sport players and their skilled moves, we cheer performers and their abilities, we eulogize each other, why shouldn't we spend even more time praising our Creator, Lord of the universe, Redeemer as well as our Saviour, Lord, Bridegroom, and our soon-coming King?

Jesus confirms that we must give such praise. "When He came near the place where the road goes down the Mount of Olives, the whole crowd of disciples began *joyfully to praise God in loud voices* for all the miracles they had seen: 'Blessed is the King who comes in the name of the Lord! Peace in heaven and glory in the highest!' Some of the Pharisees in the crowd said to Jesus, 'Teacher, rebuke Your disciples!' 'I tell you,' He replied, 'if they keep quiet, the stones will cry out'" (Luke 19:37-40).

Praise Magnifies the Lord

When we do as Psalm 34:3 says, "O magnify the Lord with me" (AMP), what do we do? Magnifying something increases the size of it. Of course, we cannot increase the size of or the actual importance of our Lord except in our own awareness. And that is what we do when we magnify the Lord. We lift Him up in our lives. As we lift Him up and look to Him, we are delivered from a low level of living which is characterized by grumbling, complaining, discouragement, and despair to a higher level of living with Him. "Just as Moses lifted up the snake in the desert, so the Son of Man must be lifted up" (John 3:14). (Also see Numbers 21:4-9.)

Magnifying an object bridges the gap that separates and draws it closer. Should an airplane fly over my home, all I would know about it would be that it was an airplane. However, if I use a good set of binoculars, I'd be able to recognize the kind of plane, its color, and maybe even something about the people in it. The binoculars allow me to cut out the foreground, blur out the background, and center on the object of attention.

When we magnify the Lord through praise that is exactly what we do. We ignore how we feel, where we are, and the way things seem—and reach to where He is. By reaching to where He is, we are lifting Him up in our lives, allowing His sustaining power and might to flow through us. This brings life-changing results within us as we honor and glorify His holy name!

HYMERA COMM. LIBRARY

Words of Praise

"I want to praise my Lord, but how do I begin? What do I say?" There is no better way to praise God than as the saints before us did. Use the words of praise recorded in His Word to lift up your inner being to Him. Consider memorizing sections like 1 Chronicles 29:11-13 and praising Him with these verses. "Yours, O Lord, is the greatness, and the power, and the glory, and the victory, and the majesty; for all that is in the heavens and the earth is Yours; Yours is the kingdom, O Lord, and Yours it is to be exalted as head over all. Both riches and honor come from You, and You reign over all. In Your hand are power and might; in Your hand it is to make great and to give strength to all. Now therefore, our God, we thank You and praise Your glorious name and those attributes which that name denotes" (AMP).

Scripture lists some of the specific things for which we are to praise our Lord. "Men shall speak of the might of Your tremendous and terrible acts, and I will declare Your greatness. They shall pour forth the fame of Your great and abundant goodness, and shall sing aloud of Your rightness and justice. They shall speak of the glory of Your kingdom and talk of Your power, to make known to the sons of men God's mighty deeds, and the glorious majesty of His kingdom" (Ps. 145:6-7, 11-12, AMP).

The Psalms are especially rich in praise. Read through them, marking those verses that express your heart's desire and give them back to Him in praise. Consider Psalms 145—150. Mary's words of praise to God (Luke 1:46-55) are also uplifting and appropriate for us to say to our Lord.

Praise Decentralizes Self

Our Lord commands us to praise Him because He knows how much it will do for us. Praise helps us become occupied with Him, which was how we were created to live rather than being preoccupied with ourselves.

Praise breaks the chains of self that wrap around us choking out life and bringing with it self-destruction. It dispels self-pity, defensiveness, and hostility. One cannot praise and sulk. Praise and grumbling, complaining and irritation cannot coexist.

Praise Increases Faith

Praise stirs up and builds our faith. In the beginning, our praise may be that of simple obedience. But as we continue to praise Him, something wonderful happens to our confidence in our relationship with God. We begin to believe what we're saying. We're raised out of the density of unbelief to see the invisible. We become aware that God is, in fact, what we are declaring—our Lord. There is a drawing together of our spirit and His Spirit. Our faith is strengthened. Our worship is strengthened. Our whole being is strengthened.

"Praise is the spark plug of faith. It is the one thing needed to get faith airborne, enabling it to soar above the deadly miasma of doubt. Praise is the detergent which purifies faith and purges doubt from the heart. The secret of faith without doubt is praise." [1]

Faith is activated through spoken words. When we verbalize what we know to be true, it is like saying the "Amen" to the fact and joining hands with God to bring it about. Thus it is necessary that we say our praises out loud and not just think them. "There is a difference between thinking and thanking. We see this in our day-to-day relationships. You may be sincerely grateful for something, but until you express your gratitude to the giver, something is missing, incomplete. Similarly, praise is not just a heart attitude, it is the expression of praise." [2]

Our praises are to be verbal. "Through Him then, let us continually offer up a sacrifice of praise to God, that is, the *fruit of lips that give thanks* to His name" (Heb. 13:15, NASB). Begin your praise each morning with verbal expression. Should you not feel the liberty to do so before your family, you can always praise while running water in the bathroom or in some other protective place.

Praise Develops Character

Just as the exercise of a muscle makes it stronger, so our character is either being strengthened toward godliness daily or being conformed to this world. "Therefore, I urge you, brothers, in view of God's mercy, to offer your bodies as living sacrifices, holy and pleasing to God—which is your spiritual worship. Do not conform any longer to the pattern of this world, but be transformed by the renewing of your mind" (Rom. 12:1-2).

Anytime we embrace suggestions or doubts that accuse God of unfaithfulness and treachery, our characters deteriorate. In the same way any antagonism, hostility, and resistance against God exercises and strengthens all that is opposed to God within us. Whereas if we receive misfortune, affliction, or sorrow from God's hand and praise Him that nothing intrinsically evil can ever come to us, our character is strengthened and reinforced toward godliness. Such praise is recognizing and bowing down to God's sovereign control. By meeting all occasions, especially adversity, with praise we are left stronger in faith, courage, and knowledge of God.

Paul and Silas exercised their character through praise during their imprisonment in Philippi. They were stripped and beaten with wooden whips till the blood ran down their bare backs. Then they were placed in the inner dungeon of the prison with their feet clamped in stocks, but they didn't whine or complain. Instead they sat there in the dungeon with the blood stiffened on their sore backs, unable to stretch their aching legs, and sang hymns of praise to God.

Then suddenly, at midnight, the chains that had bound them lay powerless behind them. They were free! God's plan was in operation. Beginning with the jailer and his entire family, the people of Philippi received the Gospel (see Acts 16).

As we praise God, we must not anticipate how He will work. Paul was not always dramatically released from prison. Sometimes he stayed there for years. He suffered many other afflictions, including being stoned and left for dead and being shipwrecked. But never once did he think that God had stopped directing every incident of his life. He counted it all an opportunity to praise God.

Our God, a God who can take all "evil" including the mistakes and sins of His penitent children and use them to enhance the character of the saint, and redound to His glory as well as boomerang against Satan, is worthy of unceasing praise.[3] Praise Him and thereby allow Him to change your character from one degree of glory to another as you behold His marvelous character.

Praise Expels Evil

Praise is an excellent protection against our enemy whether that enemy is a diabolical force or our flesh. Satan craves to be worshiped, praised, and lifted up regardless of the means used. He even tried to get our Lord to worship Him. We read, "The devil took Him to a very high mountain and showed Him all the kingdoms of the world and their splendor. 'All this I will give You,' he said, 'if You will bow down and worship me.'

"Jesus said to him, 'Away from Me, Satan! For it is written: "Worship the Lord your God, and serve Him only"'" (Matt. 4:8-10).

Satan is being worshiped today through astrology, horoscopes, fortune-telling, palm reading, clairvoyance, spiritism, telepathy, black and white magic, and other related activities. Even though we should be knowledgeable about demonology, some Christians have worshiped Satan, unknowingly, by becoming occupied with demon possession, influence, or activity. The greatest protection you have from the satanic is to keep your mind on God: "Thou wilt keep him in perfect peace, whose mind is stayed on Thee" (Isa. 26:3, KJV). What better way to keep your mind on Him than through praise?

As we read through the Gospels, we see that demons could not stand to be in the presence of Jesus without being tormented. Knowing that Psalm 22:3 points out that God "inhabits the praises" of His people, we can conclude: When we praise our Lord we drive away demonic activity. His presence expels Satan. Satan is allergic to praises raised to the Lord Jesus Christ. So let us paralyze him through praise!

Whether we are beholding our God through praise or simply beholding Him, the results are the same. When we are beholding Jesus, Satan can't even look in our direction because he can't stand to look at Jesus. So the perfect antidote for dealing with our enemy is beholding our Lord.

Praise also has a way of softening our own hearts before the Lord and bringing to light any areas that should be dealt with. One great time of praise in my life was concluded by God showing me an area in which I had wronged a brother. The Lord pointed out that an adjustment had to be made. Immediately, I picked up the phone and asked permission to visit in the home. God's presence so wrapped the entire situation so as to bless me and the one to whom I went seeking forgiveness. Praise dispels all evil in a powerful way!

Preventives to Praise

Since praise is so powerful, why is it often so difficult for us to praise? Often the biggest factor is pride. To verbally praise God for the first few times can make us feel silly or self-conscious. We wonder what others will think.

The scope of pride varies. It ranges from one who has an overinflated view of his own importance to one who believes he is worthless. Regardless of the expression, the emphasis is still "I." The person has not seen that their worthiness is based completely on God's worthship, or praise would be a natural overflow.

The first time I taught on praise I shared Hebrews 13:15, pointing out that our praise must be verbal—"the fruit of our lips" (KJV). Sandra, a sophisticated professional woman shared afterwards, "I don't think I can praise out loud. Isn't it sufficient to just think it?"

"Could your problem be pride, Sandra?" I asked. Then I challenged her to break the ice the next day by forcing herself to verbally praise her Lord out loud as soon as she woke up. The next week she agreed that her problem had been pride and she had broken through that barrier.

Just as pride can block our praise, so misunderstanding others' praises can be a hindrance to us. If we are not engulfed in the same atmosphere of praise as the praiser, we could even be repelled by their worship of God. We might compare this to being offended after observing intimate lovemaking between two people who have the right to such intimacies. Yet we've witnessed something of which we are not a part and we're repulsed.

Care must be taken not to judge other children of God lest we be the losers. Michal, David's wife, fell into this trap. As David was bringing the ark of the covenant to Jerusalem, he worshipped and praised the Lord during the journey. "David danced before the Lord with all his might, and was wearing priests' clothing. But as the procession came into the city, Michal, Saul's daughter, watched from a window and saw King David leaping and dancing before the Lord; and she was filled with contempt for him.

"Michal came out to meet him and exclaimed in disgust, 'How glorious the King of Israel looked today! He exposed himself to the girls along the street like a common pervert!'

"David retorted, 'I was dancing before the Lord who chose me above your father and his family and who appointed me as leader of Israel, the people of the Lord! So I am willing to act like a fool in order to show my joy in the Lord. Yes, and I am willing to look even more foolish than this, but I will be respected by the girls of whom you spoke!'

"So Michal was childless throughout her life" (2 Sam. 6:14, 16, 20-23, LB).

Michal misjudged David because she was not caught up in praising her Lord. As a result she suffered the greatest insult a woman of her day could suffer—that of being childless.

Not only can our own inhibitions and past misunderstandings of praise or praisers block our praise, but we are often fighting the slaying of our own ego. Could this be what is meant by the "sacrifice of praise" in Hebrews 13:15? When we praise God we must die to our own judgments, opinions, and evaluations of what is right and bow down to God's opinions, choices, and judgments. Such a death is painful. However, Jesus points out that such a death is necessary if we are to enjoy life. "For whoever wants to save his life will lose it, but whoever loses his life for Me will save it" (Luke 9:24).

So a "sacrifice of praise" is given when things seem to be going wrong and we do not feel like praising. Then by faith we concede that God is both benevolent and supreme and there are no loose ends in the universe and more particularly in our personal world. With an act of our wills we lift up our voices saying, "Praise the Lord! Praise God in His sanctuary; praise Him in the heavens of His power! Praise Him for His mighty acts; praise Him according to the abundance of His greatness" (Ps. 150:1-2, AMP).

Praise—A Way of Life

Just as being filled with God's Spirit is commanded to be our way of life (Eph. 5:18), so praise is commanded as a way of life for us. "They were also to stand every morning to thank and praise the Lord. They were to do the same in the evening" (1 Chron. 23:30). The psalmist reinforces this idea. "I will extol the Lord at all times; His praise will always be on my lips" (Ps. 34:1). We are further reminded that "they who seek the Lord will praise Him" (22:26).

Praising our Lord as a way of life does not necessarily mean saying the three words, "Praise the Lord." To do so can be appropriate when it is a genuine expression from the heart. However, guard against such praise becoming a ritualistic, meaningless, repetition of words.

Praise as a way of life means that we are continually bowing down to our God as Lord of our lives, submitting to all that He brings to us with adoration and love for Him and to Him. When David was a fugitive from the wrath of Saul, he wrote, "My heart is fixed, O God, my heart is fixed: I will sing and give praise" (57:7, KJV). His praise was not based on fluctuating circumstances or ephemeral emotional states. It was based on obedience to His God. Likewise, our praise is to be a full-time occupation.

Our Lord deserves our praise and we need the experience and blessing of praising Him. Therefore, let us lift our voices to heaven and join in with the heavenly chorus as we praise Him! What a beautiful way to join heaven and earth and at the same time to behold Him and know His overflowing joy!

Notes

[1] Paul E. Billheimer, *Destined for the Throne* (Fort Washington, PA: Christian Literature Crusade), p. 126. Chapter 8 of this inspiring book was very influential on my thoughts in this chapter on praise.

[2] E. Judson Cornwall, *Let Us Praise* (Plainfield, NJ: Logos International), p. 90. Other portions of this excellent book have contributed to this chapter as well. His other books such as *Let Us Abide, Let Us Be Holy, Let Us Enjoy Forgiveness, Let Us Draw Near, Let Us See Jesus* have also been a blessing to me.

[3] Billheimer, *Destined for the Throne* , p. 125.

Summary

To behold God by living in an awareness of His presence and to know His deep abiding peace and unfading joy means we:

1. Receive each and every thing that comes to us as from Him (Acts 17:28).
2. Vent to Him our pent-up emotions and hateful feelings about what is happening (1 Peter 5:7).
3. Confess our discouragement, self-pity, resentment, resistance, rebellion or any sin that has been exposed and receive His cleansing, based on His work at the cross on our behalf (1 John 1:9).
4. Forgive with an act of our will those who have offended or hurt us and take any steps necessary to restore the relationship (Col. 3:13).
5. Humbly cast ourselves into God's hands as putty to be molded as *He* wills! He is the Creator; we are the creatures. We melt before Him in total abandonment, relinquishing all to Him and His control (James 4:6-7; Ps. 144:15).
6. Thank God, with an act of our will till we can choose to and then delight in doing so, for each and every thing that is in our lives (1 Thes. 5:18).
7. Raise our voices to God in praise for who He is (based on His attributes) and for His mighty works (Ps. 145:1-2, 10).

HYMERA COMM. LIBRARY

Recommended Reading

Alexander, Myrna. *Behold Your God*. Grand Rapids: Zondervan.

Chapian, Marie. *Of Whom the World Was Not Worthy*. Minneapolis: Bethany Fellowship.

DeHaan, M. R. *Broken Things*. Grand Rapids: Zondervan.

Eareckson, Joni and Estes, Steve. *A Step Further*. Grand Rapids: Zondervan.

Hurnard, Hannah. *Kingdom of Love*. Wheaton: Tyndale.

Hurnard, Hannah. *Winged Life*. Wheaton: Tyndale.

Marshall, Catherine. *Something More*. Old Tappan, N. J.: Spire Books.

Packer, J. I. *Knowing God*. Downers Grove, Ill.: InterVarsity Press.

Pentecost, J. Dwight. *The Glory of God*. Portland: Multnomah Press.

Pink, Arthur W. *The Attributes of God*. Grand Rapids: Baker Book House.

Smith, Hannah Whithall. *The God of All Comfort*. Chicago: Moody Press.

Taylor, Dr. & Mrs. Howard. *Hudson Taylor's Spiritual Secret*. Chicago: Moody Press.

Tozer, A. W. *The Knowledge of the Holy*. Lincoln, Neb.: Back to the Bible Broadcast.

Tozer, A. W. *The Pursuit of God*. Wheaton: Tyndale.